# Local History

*publications from*
Neil Richardson

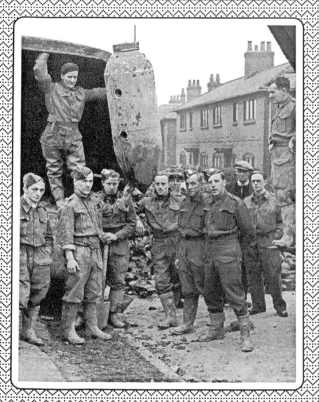

**2003-2004**

Copyright © Carnegie Publishing, 1997
Text copyright © Ann Brooks and Bryan Haworth, 1997

First published in 1997 by
Carnegie Publishing Ltd
18 Maynard Street, Preston

Typeset by Carnegie Publishing
Printed and bound by Cambridge University Press

British Library Cataloguing-in-Publication Data
A catalogue record for this book is available from the British Library

ISBN 1-85936-034-3

# Contents

# Acknowledgements

We owe a special debt to the staff and Governors of Chetham's Hospital and Library, and the committee and staff of the Portico Library for their generosity in allowing us permission to reproduce the material in this book.

We wish also to thank Adrian Wilson, Manchester Evening News, Manchester Ship Canal Company, and Quarry Bank Mill Trust.

We feel the book ought to be dedicated to J. Kohl, whose lively comments on his visit to Manchester provided the inspiration for this anthology. Finally, we must thank yet again the patient members of our families for their help and support, especially Jane Maher, who proofread the text.

## Sources of illustrations

The authors wish to thank the following for their permission to reproduce illustrations: the Governors of Chetham's Hospital and Library, Punch, Manchester Evening News, Portico Library, Adrian Wilson. The source of each illustration is given in the caption.

While every effort has been made by the authors to trace the present copyright holders we apologise in advance for any unintentional omission or error and will be pleased to insert the appropriate acknowledgements in any subsequent edition.

# Introduction

Visiting Manchester in 1841, J. F. Kohl described the city as 'mighty Manchester, with its wonders and horrors, its splendour and its misery'. This is the popular view: the pre-eminent Victorian manufacturing city of wealthy cotton merchants and dismal slums. Manchester does of course have a fascinating history prior to the industrial revolution: a history which effectively began with the building of the Roman fort at Castlefield. Manchester's past has been chronicled both by participants in events and by those looking back over time. This progress was neatly captured by a local poet:

> Once on a time this good old town was nothing
>   but a village
> of husbandry and farmers too, whose time was
>   spent in tillage:
> But things are altered very much, such building
>   not allotted is.
> It rivals far, and soon will leave behind, the
>   Great Metropolis
> O dear O, Manchester's an altered town,
>   O dear O.

An anthology can be defined as 'a choice collection', and our aim is to present such a compilation of pieces on the development of Manchester through the eyes of authors – historians, visitors and natives – both in fact and fiction. There is a wealth of material available for such a study in the many libraries and archives in the city. We have restricted the selection to the collection of the Portico Library. This Georgian building on Mosley Street holds a wonderful variety of Victorian and earlier books. Illustrations are taken from books in both the Portico and Chethams libraries. This selection has a dual advantage. First, these are the collections with which we are most familiar. Second, the book stocks, two of Manchester's hidden treasures, deserve to be better known both to the student and to the public.

The choice is a strictly personal one and does not attempt to be comprehensive nor an historical record. It reflects the interests and idiosyncrasies of the authors who have restricted the choice to works published before 1914. The authors take all responsibility for the selection though the aim has been, where possible, to use material not usually seen. Our particular thanks must go to the German visitor Kohl whose detailed report of his visit to Manchester was the stimulus for our research.

The first two chapters of the book are a pageant of Manchester history from Roman times to the beginning of the twentieth century; there then follows a grand tour of the town. Though the book is 'historical' it is hoped that it is also entertaining both to students of local history, native Mancunians, visitors and to all readers who are curious to know more about this city – Manchester.

# CHAPTER I

# 'O Manchester! How happy!'

## *How It All Began*

When entering for the first time a town like that of Manchester, a stranger, overwhelmed by the new and interesting spectacle presented to him, scarcely dares to look this giant full in the face at once, and prefers becoming gradually acquainted with some of the details before venturing to make a general survey of the whole.

(Kohl, *Ireland, Scotland and England*)

The modern visitor, like Kohl in the nineteenth century, overwhelmed by the 'new and interesting spectacle' would have difficulty finding the 'details' of the original Manchester. Throughout the town's history natives and visitors have tried to give expression to the spirit of the place,

searching the past for traces of its appeal. This interest in the eighteenth century centred on the physical remains of the Roman settlement which may still be seen at Castlefield.

Horsley, writing in 1800, reminisced:

When I was at Manchester, I examined with care the Roman station itself. It is about a quarter of a mile out of the town, being south or southwest from it. The station now goes by the name of *Giant's Castle* or *Tarquin's Castle*, and the field in which it stands is called *Castle Field*. The river runs near it on the south-east side. The ramparts are still very conspicuous.

(quoted in Watkin, *Roman Lancashire*)

Manchester 1797
(Chethams, Assheton Tonge Collection)

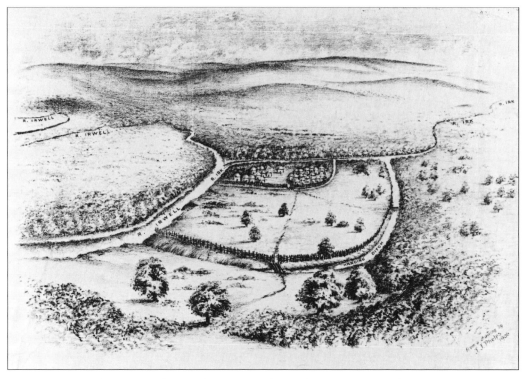

Left: Conjectural view of Mamucium, from a drawing by J. J. Phelps, 1900
(Chethams, Manchester Scrapbook)

Roman Remains
(Watkin, *Roman Lancashire*)

Antiquarians were eager to speculate on what might have been in order to explain what remained. Whitaker, writing in 1771, was typical of the writers of the period. Here he describes the founding of the town as he imagined it:

Upon this plat [plateau], then in the depth of the extensive wood of Arden, were the Sistuntii of this region induced by Agricola to erect a town. Thus induced, they felled the trees which from the first possession of the island had been the only tenants of the soil. They laid open the area, then first laid open, to the influence of the sun and winds. And they constructed their houses with timber . . .

Such was the spot which Agricola selected for the position of the town of *Mancunium*. And such was the commencement of a town that was to become so conspicuous afterwards, to lengthen out into fair streets, and to open into graceful squares, to contain assembled thousands

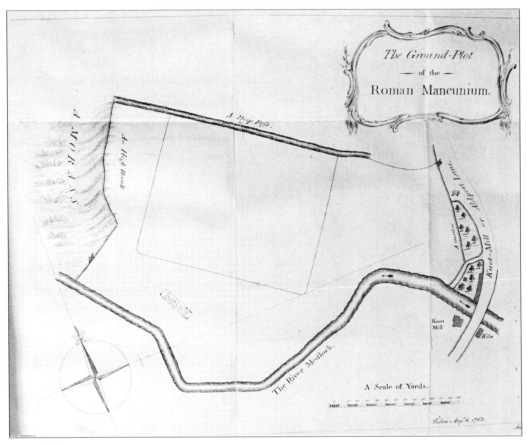

Plan of Roman Manchester
(Whitaker, *The History of Manchester*)
'. . . his newly invented map of the original town of Manchester, delineated with as much minuteness and particularity, as if he had measured the streets, built the town, and plann'd the summer station; all which curious things (if ever they existed but in his own fancy) *must* be above 1400 years before this author was born.' ('Bobbin', *Complete Works*. Remarks on Whitaker's *History of Manchester*)

within her ample circuit, and to extend her varied commerce beyond the barriers of the ocean.

(Whitaker, *History of Manchester*)

A more balanced account appeared in Watkin's *Roman Lancashire* in 1883:

The Roman *castrum* at Manchester was, like most other Roman fortresses, situated on a *lingula*, or tongue of land, formed by a curve of the river Medlock. The river approached nearest to the fortress at the southern edge of the latter, from which it was distant about eighty-five feet, forming a defence on the south-western side, a par-

tial one on the south-eastern, and a more distant one on the north-western. The river Irwell, running north and south, approaches nearest to the *castrum* opposite its western angle, from which it is distant about 528 yards, the junction with the Medlock with it occurring some 130 yards lower down . . .

The fortress occupied a slightly elevated plateau, which had a gentle slope towards the south. In the shape it was a parallelogram, the angles of which almost exactly faced the cardinal points [of the compass].

The Reverend Whitaker had very definite ideas about the layout of the Roman settlement:

Antiquarians
(Grose, *The Antiquarian Repertory*)

. . . every town must necessarily have had a market, and Manchester must have been a market-town from the first actual moment of its commencement. But the streets of Mancunium must have been all of them narrow. The first original street being constructed along the margin of the Roman road, the breadth of the latter must have been actually the width of the former. That I have previously mentioned to have been only about five yards in breadth. And the other streets of the town would certainly not be constructed of a greater, would probably not be constructed of an equal breadth. The streets of Rome were very narrow in general . . . Such therefore must have been the streets of Mancunium, and the same inconvenient narrowness has continued nearly to the present century in all the subsequent streets of Manchester. These were all certainly paved by the Roman Britons.

On this fanciful reconstruction, Tim Bobbin, the famous Lancashire humorist had some scathing comments to make:

'Manchester *must* have been a market-town, from the first *actual* moment of its commencement.' All other market towns have a kind of natural growth . . . but we find Manchester was not subject to these dilatory modes of coming to perfection. O Manchester! – how happy art thou in thy almighty antiquarian! who elucidates such profound secrets of art and nature! 'who lays open the causes and circumstances of such momentous events,' and says; Let there be a market-town; – and lo! – one starts up!

(Tim Bobbin, *Collected Works*)

For the Roman town there was evidence on the ground, but from then until the sixteenth century there are only glimpses of its development. Once again it is Whitaker who provides an insight into Saxon Manchester with a plan of the town in 627; described by Harland in 1866:

On the opposite or west side of Deansgate, in a semicircular enclosure, stands a long low dwelling of one storey, close to the line of a street, and named 'The Parsonage House'. The site is supposed to be that where the *Manchester Gazette* was first published by the late Mr Cowdroy. Three large fields between it and west side of Deansgate, and the river Irwell, are called 'The Parsonage Fields'. At the left, or north corner, at the foot of the plan we find . . . a representation of the river Irwell, where 'the great fosse' is depicted as falling into it: but later Mr Whitaker in MS corrections altered the title of 'great fosse' to 'Hanging Ditch' with its Hanging Bridge and gateway . . .

(*Collectanea*)

Evidently even Whitaker's confidence failed him, and we perhaps ought to leave him with the comments of a rival historian and antiquarian, Gough:

The least that can be said of this fantastic work, as singular for its hypothesis as its style . . . is, that the author, if he is not a Pythagorean Metempsychosist,* cotemporary [sic] with the first inhabitants of his

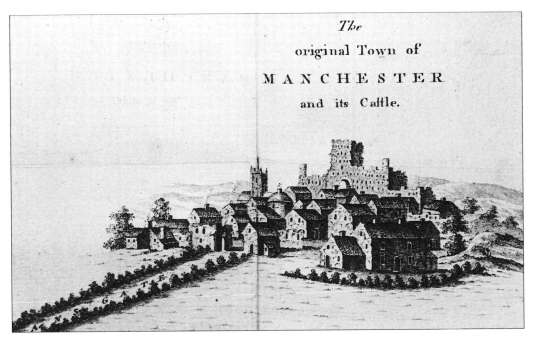

*The*

original Town of

MANCHESTER

and its Caſtle.

Manchester *c.* 627
(Whitaker, *The History of Manchester*)

favourite Mancunium, must have derived the information, which he deals out so affirmatively, from materials which his antiquarian brethren are not allowed access to, or have never dreamt of.

(*British Topography*)

★ i.e. believer in the transmigration of souls.

There is little mention of Manchester in the chronicles of the middle ages. It appears briefly in the troubled times of the Danish invasions, here recorded by the sixteenth century writer, William Camden:

A.D. 920 Edward the elder, as Marianus relates, Sent an army of Mercians into Northumberland (this town then belonging to the kings of Northumberland) to 'rebuild the town of Manchester, and place a garrison there'. For it seems to have been ruined in the Danish war; and the inhabitants say their town had its name from their brave stand against those invaders, Manchester signifying, according to them, the *city of men*, and they are won-

derfully proud of an opinion so much to their honour.

(*Britannia*, 1806 edn)

Manchester and Salford are, of course, mentioned in the Domesday survey of the late eleventh century, but a more detailed enquiry carried out a century later in 1282 provides an insight into the rural aspect of what was little more than a medieval village:

the herbage with the fruit [in the] gardens of the manor [house] of *Mamecestre* are worth yearly iis. [2 shillings]. And there is in the same place a certain little park, which is called *Alde-Parc* and *Lithe-ak*; of which the herbage with the pannage [is. worth] xxxiijs. iiijd. [33s. 4d.].

And there is there a certain other park, which is called *Blake-ley*, of which the herbage,★ with the wind-fall wood pannage † and aery of sparrow-hawks are worth yearly vil xiijs. iiijd. [£6 13s. 4d.] . . . And there is in the aforesaid manor one watermill, which is worth yearly xvijl vis iiijd [£17 6s. 4d.], and a

5

*Above*: Anglo-Saxon ladies hawking
*Right*: An Anglo-Norman House
( Both from Wright, *Homes of Other Days*)

fulling-mill, which is worth yearly xxvis. viijd. [26s. 8d.].

(Harland, *Mamecestre*)

★ herbage was the right to pasture cattle
† pannage was the right to pasture pigs in forest

Familiar names are beginning to appear among the 'herbage and pannage' but hawks being kept for hunting in Blakeley conjures up a strange picture! The modern congested city is difficult to imagine in this country setting – but it was beginning: in 1227 a charter was granted confirming an annual fair:

For ROBERT GRESLAY: Henry, King, &c., greeting. Know ye that we have granted, and by this our present Charter have confirmed, to Robert Greslay, that he and his heirs may have for ever one fair at his manor of Mamecestre, yearly, during three days, namely, on the Eve and on the Day, and on the Morrow of St. Matthew the Apostle [20 to 22 September] . . . Wherefore we will and strictly command that the said Robert and his heirs may have for ever the said fair, well and in peace, freely, quietly and honorably . . .

(*Mamecestre*)

In order to imagine the scene in medieval times historians again have to resort to flights of fancy like those of Reverend Whitaker – in 1856, J. T. Danson described the panorama of the Manchester plain in picturesque detail:

On a fine clear morning some 520 years ago – the sunlight being thrown to the north-west – the view from Blackstone Edge, over the site of this district must have presented an almost unbroken expanse of wood and waste. Its human inhabitants were few, and even less visible by their works than the same number would be now. The enclosures were very few, and the half timbered, or wattled, houses of the time, were less easily distinguished at a distance than the stone or brick edifices of a later date; and when grouped together, their fires, fed almost exclusively with wood, cast into the air no cloud of lingering smoke to mark the whereabouts of the town.'

(Danson, *On the Area*)

By 1530, when John Leland visited the town, it was a flourishing market and commercial centre:

*Mancestre* on the South Side of the Irwel River stondith in Salfordshiret, and is the fairest, best buildied, quikkest, and most populus Tounne of al *Lancastreshire*. Yet is in hit but one Paroch Chirch, but is a College and almost thoroughowt doble bilyd *ex quadrate lapide durissimo* [built of the hardest square stone], whereof a

6

An imaginative reconstruction of Manchester's Tudor buildings at the Exhibition of Manchester and Salford

(Darbyshire, *The Book of Olde Manchester and Salford*)

goodly Quarre is hard by the Towne. Ther be divers stone Bridgis in the Towne, but the best of iii Arches is over *Irwel*. This Bridge devidith *Manchestre* from *Salford*, the wich is as a large Suburbe to *Manchestre*. On this Bridg is a praty litle Chapel. The next is the Bridge that is over *Hirke* River, on wich the fair buidid College standith as in the veri Point of the Mouth of hit. For hard therby it rennith into *Wyver*. On *Hirk* River be divers fair Milles that serve the Toune. In the Towne be ii fair Market Placys.

And almost ij flyte Shottes [bow shots] withowt the Towne beneth the same syde of *Irwel* yet be seene the Dikes and Fundations of *Old Man Castel* yn a Ground inclosd.

The Stones of the Ruines of this Castel wer translated toward making of Bridgges for the Toune.

(Leland, *Itinerary*)

Another sixteenth-century visitor was William Camden, who was equally impressed:

At the confluence of the Irwell and Irk, on the left bank, which is of reddish stone, scarce three miles from the Mersey, stands that antient town called by Antoninus, MANCUNIUM and MANUCIUM, and by at present with some traces of the old name *Manchester*. This surpasses the neighbouring towns in elegance, populousness, a woollen manufacture, market, church and college founded by Lord La Ware, who took orders, and was the last male heir of his family in Henry V.

(Britannia)

It was still a rural community, as is shown in the records of orchards and gardens along Deansgate — and pigs apparently everywhere:

2 Oct. 1566

Also we find, that John Glover hathe

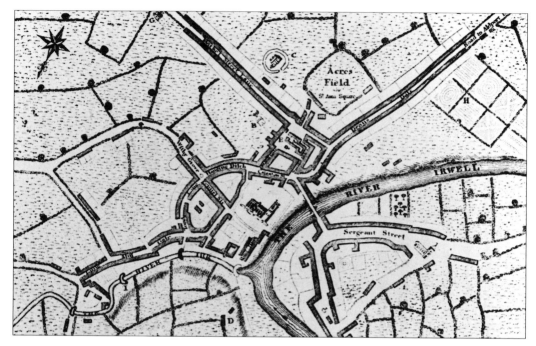

Plan of Manchester and Salford taken about 1650
(Chethams, Assheton Tonge Collection)

purchased of Thomas Tetlowe too burgags too Orchardes and too Gardins lyenge in the Denisgate in Mamchr afore this tyme in ffee ferme for Everr . . .

Also we order that every p[er]son wthin this towne shall kepe their Swine in the night tyme in some laufull Swyne Coote, So that in no wise the same swine do not go abrode in the night or lye in the churche yarde at any tyme hereafter.

*(Court Leet records)*

However 'fair' and 'elegant' Leland and Camden found it, to modern noses the town would have been less attractive:

26 March 1573
The Jurie dothe psent Robert Hulme that whereas he was appoyted to have made a pale [fence] alonge his mydinge [midden] in the fenell streete so that the said mydinge should not be noysom unto the inhabytance or passers by . . . wee order the saide Roberte to make or cause to be made a sufficient pale or wall so that the

saide mydinge be not noysom . . . The Jury Dothe psent the wiffe of James Webster that she hathe not observed An order made concerninge a certayne pryvye in a gutter therefore she is amersied [fined] iijs iiijd [3s. 4d.]

*(Court Leet records)*

It was possible for the town's population to escape from the 'noysom' smells of ill-kept middens and privies in the traditional manner – to the pub:

26 March 1573
The moste parte of the Jurie dothe thincke xxxti [thirty] Alehowses and Inns to be sufficient in Manchester.

*(Court Leet records)*

It would be interesting to know whether the rest of the jury thought there were too few or too many!

A century later Dr Kuerden was happy to repeat Camden's praise of the town:

The town is pleasantly situated, and, as

8

Mr Cambden sayth, excelleth all the towns about it, and it is the fayrest and most populous in all the county, hath many streets, and a spacious market-place; a church collegiate with a Mr Warden and fellows, two chaplains, organ, singing men, quorister boys, a colldg in it, with a sumpts library . . . Manchester is a fayre built town, more citty like than any other town or borow in the county of Lancaster, being of great antiquity amongst the Brigantes in the British time.

(quoted in Baines, *History and Gazetteer*)

The town had changed little over the years and was still rural in character as a later investigation of the common field system showed:

Acres field lay somewhere about Quay Street. How far north of that street it extended is unknown, but probably Quay Street now forms the site of the hedge that was the southern boundary of the field. The next known point north of Quay Street is Spinning-field, the north side of which is now represented by Wood Street, to the north again of which was a field bearing the significant name of 'Dolefield,★ still perpetuated by a street of that name, running south from Bridge Street. 'Dolefield' seems to imply that in former times it was owned or occupied in strips . . . From that it might easily pass into a state of market gardens, and in 1650, a map of Manchester shows this particular piece of land, from Deansgate to the Irwell, as a succession of gardens.

(Danson, *On the area*)

★ 'dole' was a portion of land 'doled' out to an individual.

The fields and gardens of seventeenth-century Manchester could lend themselves to the same sort of fanciful reconstruction as the medieval landscape. Here is another highly romantic view written in 1880:

for what the town was in 1650, it would be in 1640, and probably for two centuries or more before that. It will represent not only what Manchester was in the wars of the Commonwealth, but in the wars of the Roses, when the little old town had its one single Church, its one bridge over the Irwell, gliding clear and pleasantly by, the pellucid water inhabited by innumerable trout, and probably well stocked with salmon, in their season; its houses all of wood and plaster, low roofed and of many gables, from whose projecting upper stories the maidens could send a greeting across the narrow streets in the early morn, and neighbours could hold converse from their doors; from the oriels and bays at the back of which, lighting their pleasant sitting-rooms, were views of the gardens and orchards which stretched away towards the fields; for nearly every house had its garden and orchard; to these continual reference is made in old documents. No doubt the ceilings of the houses were low, and the rooms small; the streets narrow, ill-paved, and worse lighted; and when a fire broke out it was with difficulty extinguished; but there must have been much that was pleasant about the old town. All around it were beautiful parks and bosky woods.

(Procter, *Bygone Manchester*)

There is no room in Procter's idyllic picture for the stinking refuse heaps of actuality.

Yet things were improving: in 1536 a public water supply was set up with a conduit in the market place, fed from the spring in Spring Gardens. But again there were problems – by the 1640s things were going wrong:

19 October 1647
The Jury doth order that the Officers appoynted for the lookinge to the Conduit and the Conduit Head shall forthwith take a view of the decayes of them and provyde for the speedie decayes [mistake for 'repairs'] of the wants of them . . . And it is further ordered That whereas diverse servants have broken of the Locks & with stones have broken the Cockes to

The Conduit
No picture is known of the conduit. This is Nathan Compton's folly, representing the conduit, in the Exhibition of Manchester and Salford.
(Darbyshire, *The Book of Olde Manchester and Salford*)

'It was forbidden in 1585 to wash clothes, scour vessels, or cleanse "meats of beasts" or calves at this, the chief source of the water supply of the town.'
(Axon, *Annals of Manchester*)

make the Conduit out of order that the masters of such servants & the p[ar]ents of such Children as shal be found offendinge in the pmisses shall make satisfaccon for defaults as the overseers of the Conduit shall thincke fit . . .

(*Court Leet records*)

A few years later, to celebrate the coronation of Charles II there were no complaints about the functioning of the conduit:

7 May 1661
[A procession 'with the Town-Musick playing before upon loud instruments' paraded through the town] and so forwards to the Conduit Officers and Souldiers in their orders; the Gentlemen and Officers drunck his Majesties health in Claret running forth at three streames of the said Conduit, which was answered from the Souldiery by a great volley of shot, and many great shouts, saying, *God save the King*: which being ended, the Gentry and Ministers went to Dinner, attended with the Officers and Musick of the Town; the Auxilliaries dineing at the

same place; during the time of dinner and until after Sun-set, the said Conduit did run with pure Claret, which was freely drunke by all that could, for the croud come near the same.

(*Court Leet Records*)

By the eighteenth century the modern town was beginning to take shape, still primarily a market town but now bustling with new commerce. William Stukeley, yet another antiquarian tourist, visited Manchester in 1776:

I look upon Manchester to be no ancient town; and even the hundred is denominated from Saltford, the village on the other side of the bridge, therefore older: but Manchester is a much better situation, as higher; placed too between two rivers, having rocky and precipious banks, with a good prospect: it is a very pleasant, large, populous, and thriving town; new buildings added every day: the roads are mending about it, and the river is making navigable; which will still contribute to its prosperity. The old church is very spacious and handsome, and enlarged still with

A View of the Old Coffee House
(Chethams, Manchester Scrapbook)

numbers of large chapels and oratories; but the monuments, which were many, are destroyed and obliterate . . .

(*Itinerarium Curiosum*)

What the town was like, before the new building and the improvements of the eighteenth century, was described by 'a native of Manchester' in 1783:

Before the present avenue was opened between St Anne's-square and the Exchange the communication went under the old coffee-house fronting the Exchange, in a line with the corner shop, towards Market-street-lane – that for carriages through a narrow gateway, which was further disgraced by a cobbler's stall, and over this, by narrow stairs, in the true garret-stile, there was one way to the old coffee-house rooms above, those below being let for shops. There was just room for foot-passengers to avoid carriages on that side where the stairs stood, by keeping in line with them, and bolting through the gateway

when there was an opportunity. The other communication from the Market-place (to the square) for the people on foot, was through an entry which led to the great stairs of the old coffee-house, and across a small court where a pump stood, at the head of the only passage this way; which was so gloomy and dismal, even at noon day, that it deservedly acquired the name of '*the Dark-entry*'.

(quoted in Baines, *History and Directory*)

By the end of the century Manchester was entering into that period of expansion which was to make it second only to the capital itself. The historians of the time could not agree on its origins, or even its original name, but there was a pervading feeling of optimism and trust in the future best summed up in the statistics gathered by Aiken in his monumental *A description of the country from thirty to forty miles around Manchester.*

In 1773 a survey of Manchester was executed with accuracy, which gave the following results:

|                    | Manchester | Salford | Total |
| ------------------ | ---------- | ------- | ----- |
| Houses (inhabited) | 3402       | 866     | 4268  |
| Families           | 5317       | 1099    | 6416  |
| Male inhabitants   | 10548      | 2248    | 12796 |
| Female ditto       | 11933      | 2517    | 14450 |
| Both sexes         | 22481      | 4765    | 27246 |

Persons to a house, 6⅓ To a family, 4¼ . . .

At Christmas 1788, the numbers by enumeration were, in the township of Manchester, 5961 houses, 8570 families, 42,821 persons; in the township of Salford, about 1260 houses. The whole number of people in both towns might then be reckoned at more than 50,000.

During the year 1791, the christenings in these towns amounted to 2,960; the burials to 2268. These numbers, by the usual mode of calculating, will give from sixty-five to seventy-four thousand inhabitants – an increase almost unparalleled!

Southerly view of Market Street, 1820
(Chethams, Assheton Tonge Collection)

As the new century dawned the prospects looked bright, but what was to become of the 'pelucid' Irwell, the 'old church' and 'Tarquin's Castle'?

The new buildings, the expanding commerce and the growing population were to change the face of the town for ever.

# CHAPTER 2

# 'Manchester's Improving Daily'

## Into The Nineteenth Century

*Oh, this Manchester's a famous town,*
*The great Metropolis of Trade, Sirs,*
*And it still is rising in renown,*
*By th' great improvements daily made, Sirs,*
*All strangers view it with surprise, Sirs,*
*And townsfolk scarce believe their eyes, Sirs,*
*But looking round cry out quite gaily*
*Lord, Manchester's improving daily.*
*Sing high, sing low, sing hey down gaily,*
*Manchester's improving daily.*

(Lancashire folk song, *c.* 1840)

In 1895 B. A. Redfern in his biography of Charles Wareing Bardsley, a Manchester cleric, imagined Manchester's topographical situation at the beginning of the nineteenth century:

> The traveller from the south who had just crossed the Cheshire plain would here come upon one of those lands of the lower foot-hills, such as always afford the most varied scenery – a country of irregularly-rounded grass slopes, with occasional broken cliffs, intersected by a few open dales and many well-wooded cloughs, along which ran the numerous rills or streams carrying tribute to the Irwell . . . here in the Irwell basin a traveller might for a season possess his soul in peace

Manchester from Kersal Moor
(Chethams, Assheton Tonge Collection)

St Peter's Church, Manchester
(Everett, *Manchester Guide*)

above the great floods, below the great winds; in a pleasant land, equally removed from tameness and from savagery.

(Manchester Literary Club)

In reality by 1795, Manchester was indeed a small town surrounded by countryside, but growing fast, as Aiken describes:

Manchester and Salford, in several streets and the market place, bear great marks of antiquity, as there are still standing nearly whole streets of houses built of wood, clay, and plaster.

The new streets built within these few years have nearly doubled the size of the town. Most of them are wide and spacious, with excellent and large houses, principally built of brick made on the spot; but they have a flight of steps pro-

jecting nearly the breadth of the pavement, which makes it very inconvenient to foot passengers . . . In the first year after obtaining the act for lighting and paving the town, a considerable debt was incurred. On this account, Manchester was, as before the act, in total darkness; but by receiving the money and using no oil, the fund has recovered itself and the town is now well lighted. But very few of the streets are yet flagged, which makes the walking in them, to strangers, very disagreeable.

(*Thirty miles around Manchester*)

By 1806 its manufacturing trades were already well known nationally and the basis for future growth:

Manchester may be called the largest

village in England . . . it has the greatest trade of any inland town in these northern parts, and has had a rapid increase in the two late centuries. The fustian or cotton manufacture has been improved of late . . . and this with the great variety of other manufactures known by the name of *Manchester wares,* renders both the town and the parish and the neighbourhood for many miles round rich, prosperous, and industrious. Not to mention the many new and handsome houses from time to time rising in different parts of the town.

(Gough in Camden, *Britannia*)

The population of the town grew rapidly and was a cause for comment for both natives and visitors. Aston's guide book, *A Picture of Manchester,* in 1816 goes into great detail, allowing him to comment:

This population added to the suburb townships actually *adjoining* the town of Manchester, appearing to the eye, *one undivided* mass of building; in short, forming *one town,* as the buildings congregated at the Metropolis are called 'LONDON,' make out the assertion, that Manchester is the second town in the kingdom.

The growth was due not only to an increase in the birthrate locally but to immigrants drawn to Manchester by its industry:

. . . not one half of the adult inhabitants (perhaps not more than one-third) are natives of Manchester; every week, bringing an accession of numbers. . . The glorious results of the campaigns of 1813–4–5,⋆ having not only returned many thousands, soldiers and sailors, to their families, but also by renovating trade, have given a new spring to the prosperity of Manchester, which has brought talent, capital and industry from every part of the kingdom to profit by it.

(Aston, *Picture of Manchester*)

⋆ The campaigns of the Napoleonic wars

The population was to become even more cosmopolitan as workers were drawn in from

Warehouses, 107 Piccadilly, Manchester
(Tracy, *Port of Manchester*)

further and further afield. By 1882 Grindon could write:

The composition of the Manchester community is extremely miscellaneous. A steady influx of new-comers from all parts of Great Britain – Scotland very particularly – has been in progress for eighty or ninety years . . . and seems likely to continue. Not very long ago the suburb called Greenheys was regarded as a German colony. Many Levantine Greeks have also settled in Manchester, and of Jews the estimated number in September 1879 was ten thousand. Not withstanding the influence which these new-comers have almost necessarily, though undesignedly, brought to bear upon the general spirit of the town, the original Lancashire character is still prominent, though greatly modified, both for the better and the worse.

(*Lancashire*)

This rapid expansion of population gave rise to problems, not only of housing and health, but also the provision of basic services which were more suited to eighteenth-century Manchester as the conduit was still the main source of domestic water:

Relatively considered, Manchester is situated on low ground: there is a descent to it, which ever way it is approached. The air is, perhaps too moist, partly owing to its situation, at the junction of three rivers; and partly to its laying so immediately in the vicinity of the range of Yorkshire hills, from which the clouds, gathered over the western ocean, are driven back into the valley; and perhaps, something ought to be attributed to the circumstances of many of the old streets being built upon morasses, and the site of old pools of water . . . There is but one draw-well in the whole town, and that, very properly, is inclosed in a building which is always locked, except when the well is in actual use. Two springs in Castle Field, which issue from the side of the brow, have the character of better water than any other wells; and are much resorted to for the tea-table . . . Almost every house of moderate size, is furnished with a lead or stone cistern, which serves as a reservoir for the rain . . . By some, this water is used not only for cleaning, but for brewing, and even for culinary purposes.

(Aston, *A Picture of Manchester*)

By 1836, water was being brought in via stone water pipes from private reservoirs about two miles outside the town. It was not until 1850 that the reservoirs at Denton and Hyde were constructed.

Joseph Aston's conclusion that 'the air is too moist' and that the situation of the town was the reason for so much precipitation was correct. One of the most persistent images of Manchester as the rainy city was well established by the 1820s. In 1821, a visitor to Manchester eloquently recorded his experiences: [see below]

Baines reports that by 1824 Mancunians were already anxious to defend their climate:

Manchester is frequently represented as under the visitation of perpetual rain, but in reality the air and the climate of this place do not in any material degree differ from other parts of the county . . . Taken on average of years, there are three wet days and four days of fair weather in a week.

(*History and Directory*)

Both Baines and our anonymous visitor agree that despite the climate Manchester was set to flourish:

The appearance of the town is continually improving, from the streets becoming more spacious and the public buildings more handsome. Prosperity, and its natural associate, contentment, prevail to an extent that has seldom been exceeded, and the indication of opulence, which exhibit themselves in a thousand different ways, become every year more decided . . . Instead of sharing the fate of a large portion of the Roman stations this place has preserved, through successive ages, its rank amongst the first of the British towns; in many of the great political events which have marked the eras of our national history, it has taken a prominent part; the

*FASHIONABLE and CHEAP PARASOL MANUFACTORY, 260, DEANSGATE.*
S. RICHARDSON returns his grateful acknowledgments to his Friends, for their kind patronage, since his commencement in business; and most respectfully acquaints the Ladies of Manchester, Salford, and the vicinity, that he has now ready for inspection, an elegant Assortment of PARASOLS, manufactured from the best materials, and such as he, with confidence, can recommend.—Wholesale orders executed on the first rate principle  All kinds of Silk and Gingham UMBRELLAS, at very low prices.—Repairs of every description punctually attended to.

*Above*: Fashionable and cheap parasol manufactory, *Courier*, 23 May 1825
*Left*: Impromptu, *Manchester Chronicle*, 8 December 1821
(Both from Chethams, Newspaper Collection)

IMPROMPTU, by a Gentleman, on quitting Manchester on a rainy day ; Saturday last.—Written at the coach-office.
    I arrived in a *show'r*, in the *wet* now set off,
        Eight days in this place I remain'd,
    Seven days seven nights and a quarter, I vow,
        By Jove ! it incessantly RAIN'D.
    What then ? not a day nor an hour was I dull :
        The Lancashire lads play'd their parts :
    I found every friend of politeness brim full,
        And myself in the midst of the Arts. *
    May Manchester flourish ! and if once again
        By chance I should ere be brought hither,
    I hope that from weeping the clouds may refrain,
        And grant me a peep at fine weather.
* The Gentlemen at Manchester are particularly noted as amateurs and patrons of the fine arts.

No. I. showing the mean quantity of Rain, and number of Wet Days in Manchester, from 1807 to 1824, both inclusive:—

| January. | | February. | | March. | | April. | | May. | | June. | |
|---|---|---|---|---|---|---|---|---|---|---|---|
| Inches of Rain. | Wet Days | Inches of Rain. | Wet Days | Inches of Rain. | Wet Days | Inches of Rain. | Wet Days | Inches of Rain. | Wet Days | Inches of Rain. | Wet Days |
| 2.234 | 12 | 2.454 | 13 | 2.456 | 13 | 1.713 | 13 | 2.824 | 14 | 2.433 | 12 |

| July. | | August. | | September. | | October. | | November. | | December. | |
|---|---|---|---|---|---|---|---|---|---|---|---|
| Inches of Rain. | Wet Days | Inches of Rain. | Wet Days | Inches of Rain. | Wet Days | Inches of Rain. | Wet Days | Inches of Rain. | Wet Days | Inches of Rain. | Wet Days |
| 3.427 | 15 | 3.163 | 16 | 3.002 | 14 | 3.789 | 16 | 3.493 | 16 | 3.559 | 14 |

TABLE II. On the Temperature at Manchester, shows the general annual Mean from 1807 to 1820, both inclusive, to be 48° 87; and

TABLE III. exhibiting the Barometrical Results of the same fourteen years gives 29.75 as the General Mean; 30.669 as the greatest mean Elevation in Inches; 28.350 as the least mean Elevation; 2.314 as the difference of the extremes; 1.02 as the mean variation in twenty-four hours; 64.70 as the mean spaces in inches; and 151 as the mean number of changes per year.

The manners of the people in the manufacturing districts of the county have been already described, and the characteristics there given apply with as much force in Manchester as in any part of the county.* The appearance of the town is continually improving, from the streets becoming more spacious and the public buildings more handsome. Prosperity, and its natural associate, contentment, prevail to an extent that

* See v. i. p.141.

Chart of mean quantity of rain, and number of wet days in Manchester, from 1807 to 1824, both inclusive (Baines, *History and Directory*)

first of the staple manufactures of the kingdom has chosen this for its favourite seat; and the capability displayed by Manchester at the present moment for future growth exceeds even its past prosperity.

(*History and Directory*)

As Manchester's fame spread as the centre of industrialisation the city itself became an attraction to visitors drawn by reports of the mighty mills. Kohl, making a tour of the United Kingdom in 1841, succinctly commented:

It cannot be said that Manchester is either an ugly or a beautiful town, for it is both at once. Some quarters are dirty, mean, ugly, and miserable-looking to an extreme; others are interesting, peculiar, and beautiful in the highest degree.

(*Ireland, Scotland and England*)

Hugh Miller, visiting in 1845, felt it a true representative of England's great manufacturing towns.

One receives one's first intimation of its existence from the lurid gloom of the atmosphere that overhangs it. There is a murky blot in one section of the sky, however clear the weather, which broadens and heightens as we approach, until at length it seems spread over half the firmament. And now the innumerable chimnies come in view, tall and dim in the dun haze, each bearing atop its troubled pennon of darkness. And now we enter the suburbs, and pass through mediocre streets of brick, that seem as if they had been built wholesale by contract within the last half-dozen years. These humble houses are the homes of the operative manufacturers . . . As we advance, the town presents a new feature. We see whole streets of warehouses, — dead, dingy, gigantic buildings, barred out from the light; and, save where here and there a huge waggon stands, lading or unlading, under the mid-air crane, the thoroughfares, and especially the numerous *cul-de-sacs*, have a solitary half-deserted air. But the city clocks have just struck one — the dinner hour of the labouring English; and in one brief minute two-thirds of the population of the place have turned out into the streets. The rush of the human tide is tremendous . . . But the outburst is short as fierce: . . . in a few minutes all is over, and the streets even more quiet and solitary than before. There is an air of much magnificence about the public buildings devoted to

*Left*: Cartouche of Mill
("Alfred Arnold's Choice")
'. . . frequent buildings among them [the houses] as
large as convents, without their antiquity, without
their beauty, without their holiness; where you
hear from within, as you pass along, the everlasting
din of machinery; and where, when the bell rings it
is to call wretches to their work, instead of their
prayers . . .'
(Espriella, *Letters from England*)
*Below*: Tempest Booth Mill.
Chethams, *Business Directory*, 1868–9.)
'The earliest cotton mill built in Manchester is
commonly stated to have been erected about 1783,
in Miller-street, where the Public Baths and
Washhouses now stands.'
(Earwaker, *Local Gleanings*)

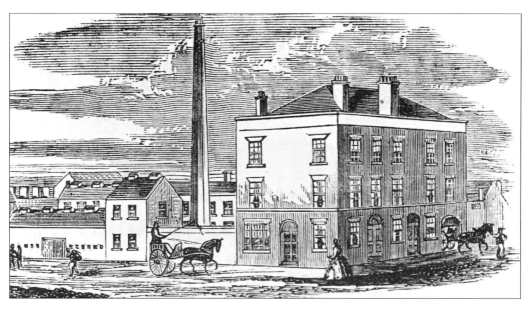

trade; and the larger shops wear the solid
aspect of long- established, well-founded
business.

(*First Impressions*)

The change had been exceedingly rapid. Compare Miller's account to that of Benjamin Love,
writing in 1839, who was still able to interview
elderly inhabitants about Manchester's appearance only thirty years previously.

They remember a time, for instance,
when Ardwick Green, now connected

by a long row of houses, was a long
country walk – when the site of the
present substantial houses in New Market
buildings was a pool of water – when
the present handsome sheet of water in
front of the Infirmary was a stagnant
pond – when Oxford-road and Lower
Mosley-street, and all the districts beyond, were yet fields and gardens . . .
They can recollect the first factory
erected in the town – the one in Miller's-lane – and the crowds of people

that flocked to see the high chimney belonging to it, when it was in the progress of erection – they remember Strangeways, when a public-house, its bowling-green, and the pile called Strangeways-hall, were the only encroachments on green fields and pastures stretching even to Hunt's-bank – they tell of the time when a coach to Liverpool started at six o'clock in the morning, and reached its destination at the same hour in the evening.

(Manchester as it is)

The locals may have flocked to that first chimney, later the curious from around the world were to flock to Manchester's smoking stacks. The industrial image is to be found, not only in travellers tales, but also in the literature of the period. W. Harrison Ainsworth used his birthplace as the setting of many of his historical novels. His imaginative description in *Mervyn Clitheroe* (1857) gives a graphic picture of Manchester, alias 'Cotton-borough', which echoes Kohl and Miller:

The Homeless Poor
(*Punch*, 1859)

What a wondrous town is Cottonborough! How vast – how populous – how ugly – how sombre! Full of toiling slaves, pallid from the close confinement and heated air. Full of squalor, vice, misery: yet full of wealth and all its concomitants – luxury, splendour, enjoyment. The city of coal and iron – the city of the factory and the forge – the city where great fortunes are amassed, and more quickly, than in any other in the wide world. But how – and at what expense? Ask your crew of care-worn men, wan women, and sickly children, and they will tell you. Look at yon mighty structure, many-windowed, tall-chimneyed, vomiting forth clouds of smoke, to darken and poison the wholesome air. Listen to the clangour and the whirl of the stupendous and complicated machinery within. Count the hundreds of pale creatures that issue forth from it at meal-times. Mark them well, and say if such employment be healthy. Yet these poor souls earn thrice the wages of the labourer at the plough, and therefore they eagerly pursue their baneful taskwork. Night comes; the mighty mill is brilliantly lighted up, and the gleam from its countless windows is seen afar. It looks like an illuminated palace . . . Ugly and black is Cottonborough, shrouded by smoke, tasteless in architecture, boasting little antiquity, and less of picturesque situation; yet not wholly devoid of a character strongly impressive . . . Prosperous is Cottonborough – prosperous beyond all other cities – and long may it continue so; for, with all its ugliness, and all its faults – and they are many – I love it well.

As the century progressed Manchester became the trading centre for the Lancashire industrial belt, and less important as a manufacturing town.

Now, the towns and villages outside are all devoted to spinning and weaving. While Liverpool is one great wharf, the middle of Manchester is one great warehouse, a reservoir for the production of

Market Street, 1820
(Ralston, *Old Manchester*)

the whole district. The trade falls under two principal heads – the Home and the Export. In either case the produce of the looms, wherever situate, is brought just as it flows from them-rough, or, technically, 'in the grey' . . . Very interesting it is to observe, in going through a great warehouse, not only how vast is the quantity waiting transfer, but how differently the various fabrics have to be folded and ornamented so as to meet the taste of the nations and foreign countries they are intended for.

(Grindon, *Lancashire*)

The nineteenth century saw Manchester change from 'the largest village in England' to 'Cottonopolis'. By the end of the century few of the population lived in the city centre, given over as it was to trade. The rich had moved, some as far as the Lancashire coast and the Lake District. The poor were still crowded around the inner city and the rest in the expanding ring of outer suburbs. This kaleidoscopic change is perhaps best exemplified by what was called 'the principal thoroughfare of the town' – Market Street, frequently described by visitors as an example of the essential Manchester.

In 1825 Baines described how it was being brought up to nineteenth-century standards:

[It] had long been inadequate to the convenient carrying on of the vast traffic with which it was continually crowded. To remedy this increasing evil, an act was passed in 1821, with the general concurrence of the town, to improve and widen Market-street to the extent of twenty-one yards . . . The Commissioners lost no time in commencing their operations; a fine spacious street, with handsome shops and dwellings on each side, descending by a regular inclined plane from Piccadilly to the Exchange, is now forming, and the

Royal Exchange, Lower Market Street
(Chethams, Assheton Tonge collection)

work has been prosecuted with so much vigour and success, that the labours of the Commissioners are expected to terminate in this quarter, in the year 1826.

(Baines, History and Directory)

Nearly twenty years later Kohl, with his stranger's eye, caught the atmosphere of this, the hub of 'the workshop of the world':

Come with me, then, dear reader, and let us take a short walk together through these various scenes. We set out from the broad, stately, and imposing Market-street, which runs from the river Irwell, right through the heart of the town, and continuing under the name of Piccadilly, loses itself in the opposite suburbs, under the third *alias* of the London-road. This street is always busy, noisy, and interesting, and contains numbers of splendid shops. In the evening, its thousands of gaslights glittering from the shops and street-lamps, make it almost painfully dazzling to the eyes not

yet accustomed to these nightly illuminations of the great English cities. In this street the beggars of Manchester love to congregate, importuning the wealthy and idle as they pass . . . Among these busy and idle crowds, numbers of hackney-coaches and cabs pursue their way, and in still greater numbers, the carts, waggons, and vans, of the merchants and manufacturers, of all sorts and sizes, hurry along.

(Ireland, Scotland and England)

By the twentieth century, the great days were passing but Williamson recorded the continuing bustle of activity:

The finest picture in Manchester is the view of Market Street looking from St Mary's Gate upwards to Piccadilly when the gray mist of a mild south-windy afternoon has melted into murky gloom. It is a scene full of light, life, movement, colour, and music-thrilling, emotional, fascinating. The serried lines of lamps

'Looking up Market Street'
(Shaw, *Manchester Old and New*)

stand like sentinels guarding the busy thoroughfare from the enveloping darkness, an enemy difficult to keep at bay. On both side brilliant windows throw warm waves of white and yellow on the wet pavement, save where the mellow rays, streaming through a chemist's tinted glass bottles, make a mosaic of blue and green and gold. Throngs of eager pedestrians hurry by, threading in and out, like motes in a sunbeam. Crowded electric cars emerge from the dusky depths of Victoria Station in constant succession, with a kling, kling of warning bells . . . Impatient motors break from the welter of traffic: dodge in front of cabs and behind trams with headlamps glaring like a monster's fiery eyes, and finally vanish round the corner with hideous hoots. Midway, but inaudible to the spectator, cheap music sellers, fruit hawkers, and the vendors of penny toys perambulate by the kerb side, to gather spoil from the pulsating tide of humanity that ceaselessly ebbs and flows.

(Williamson, 'Art in Manchester')

Manchester, as the balladeer sang, had been 'improving daily'.

# CHAPTER 3

# 'The Hapless River'

## *The Irwell*

Nothing seems more characteristic of the great manufacturing city, though disagreeably, than the river Irwell, which runs through the place, dividing it into a lesser and larger town, that though they bear different names, are essentially one.

*(First Impressions)*

This was Hugh Miller's impression of the importance of the Irwell to Manchester in 1845. Throughout its recorded history the Irwell is ever-present in descriptions of the city, and played a central role in the growth of Manchester.

The Irwell is one of the chief tributaries of the Mersey, and, though not large, is important, from its position with regard to Manchester and other large manufacturing towns of Lancashire. Its drainage area is 312 square miles, and its length of course 40 miles, chiefly through New Red Sandstone.

(Ansted, *Water and Water Supply*)

North Cut View of the Old Bridge
(Corbett, *The River Irwell*)

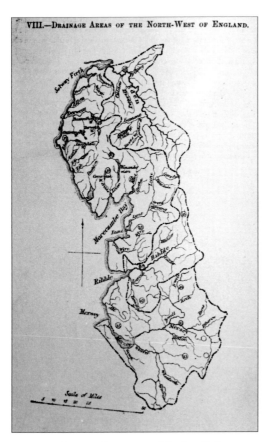

Map showing the course of the Irwell from
Drainage Areas of the North West of England.
(Ansted, *Water and Water Supply*)

A description of its course reveals just how central the river was to development of the Manchester region:

> The Irwell rises at the Erewll spring, in
> the moors a little to the east of Hasling-
> den, 1,325 feet above the sea, near the
> Old Forest of Rosendale on the borders of
> Yorkshire, and collecting several small
> feeders, flows southwards a few miles and
> receives the *Swillen Brook* from Haslingden.
> Thence it continues nearly south for six
> miles to Bury, between hills that close in
> the valley on each side, and have few
> breaks. Two miles below Bury the *Roch*
> enters on the left bank. [The Roch, after
> rising in the Pennines, passes through
> Rochdale] . . . After receiving the Roch
> the Irwell continues to flow about 3 miles

in a westerly course, and then receives the
Tonge or Croal coming in from the north-
west, and passing on its way the town of
Bolton-le-Moors . . . At the confluence of
the Tonge the Irwell makes an acute angle
with its former course, taking the direction
of the Tonge and flowing south-east to Salford and Manchester, the distance in a
straight line being about 7 miles, but in-
cluding the contortions much greater.
Winding through the western part of the
city of Manchester it receives the *Irk,* a
small feeder from the north, and the *Medlock,* another feeder from the east. It then
flows west passing through Trafford Park.
After a few miles, coasting the great flat
waste of Chat moss, it reaches the Mersey,
between Chat moss and Carrington moss.

(Ansted, *Water and Water Supply*)

Aston's description of 1816 shows that it was
still a beautiful river in parts:

> The Salford Crescent, which stands upon
> a spot almost unrivalled for a beautiful and
> commanding prospect . . . The fertile val-
> ley – the meandering of the river Irwell,
> approaching to and receding from the
> Crescent – the rural cots, the pleasant
> villas – the rising hills . . .

(*A Picture of Manchester*)

Compare this to the river which Kohl saw in
1841. Could there have been a more dramatic
change?

> We pass on to the banks of the rivers
> which run through the city. These are
> three, the Medlock, the Irk, and the
> Irwell. Here the scene varies. The rivers
> are intersected by an immense number
> of large and small bridges, in every form
> and direction. Standing upon one of
> these bridges, let us look around us a
> little. What an extraordinary spectacle!
> There stand rows and groups of huge
> manufactures, each consisting of a
> numerous buildings which are sometimes
> bound together by one surrounding wall.
> Sometimes these walls are fortified
> and guarded like fortresses, by vigilant

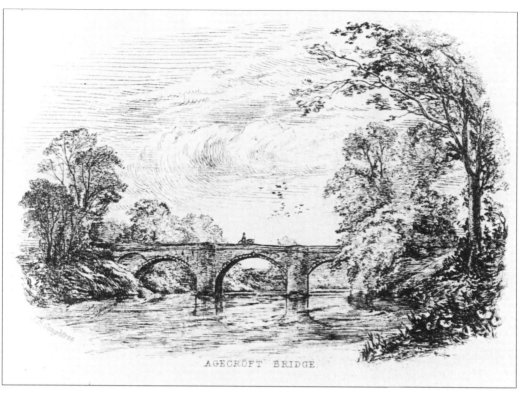

Agecroft Bridge over the Irwell
(Chethams, Assheton Tonge Collection)

View from the Crescent, Salford
(Chethams, Assheton Tonge Collection)

New Bailey Bridge, Manchester
(Chethams, Assheton Tonge Collection)

sentinels, who allow none to pass but such as have a right to enter. See how eagerly these manufactures suck up, through pumps and buckets, the river water, which dirty as it is, is invaluable to them, and which they pour back into the river, in black, brown, and yellow currents . . .

(*Ireland, Scotland and England*)

Miller, too, described the river, a river that seems to have been one of the 'tourist' sights for visitors:

The hapless river – a pretty enough stream a few miles higher, with trees over-hanging its banks, and fringes of green sedge set thick along its edges – loses caste as it gets among the mills and the print-works. There are myriads of dirty things given it to wash, and whole wag-gon-loads of poisons from dye-houses and bleach-yards thrown in to it to carry away; steam-boilers discharge into it their seething contents, and drains and sewers their fetid impurities; till at length it rolls on . . . In passing along where the river sweeps by the old Collegiate Church, I met a party of town-police dragging a fe-male culprit – delirious, dirty, and in

drink – to the Police Office; and I bethought me of the well-known comparison of Cowper, beginning
'*Sweet stream, that winds through yonder glade,*
*Apt emblem of a virtuous maid,–*'
of the maudlin woman not virtuous – and of the Irwell.

(*First Impressions*)

So the river that was described as the 'clear and winding Irwell' in the title to the print 'South West Prospect of Manchester' in 1728 was notorious just over a century later for its grimy condition in both fact and fiction.

> *Who e'er hath seen dark Irwell's tide,*
> *Its sombre look and sullen glide,*
> *Would never deem that it, I ween,*
> *Had ever brighter, gayer been . . .*
> *When Irwell rolled by feudal tower,*
> *By shady grove, and fairy bower;*
> *When on her banks so oft was borne*
> *Sweet music of the hunter's horn . . .*
> *Forests are here, but not of trees;*
> *Forests are here, the homes of men;*
> *Mancunian's sons are as the leaves*
> *Which bloomed upon the forest then*

Joseph Anthony
(Procter, *Memorials of Bygone Manchester*)

The MARY: A YARN
Air: The Ram of Derby

The Union flag is flying,
By the Company's wharf, Old Quay,
And 'Mary' of Dublin lying,
unloading her Murphies today.

And soon may scores of others
And perform the trip with her,
And trade and commerce double
In Noble Manchester

(Navigable Rivers of England, quoted in History
of the Manchester Ship Canal.)

The Old Quay, 1746
(Chethams, Manchester Scrapbook)

Manchester and Salford Regatta, 1844, from Throstle Nest showing, on the right, fields, farm building and
grandstand where the Manchester Docks are now; on the left, fields, grandstand, booths etc., where mills
and works are now
(Illustrated London News, from Corbett, The River Irwell)

The river was also one of the main thoroughfares
for passengers and heavy goods to Manchester.
The principal landing point was the Old Quay,
near Castlefield. Country people coming to
Manchester travelled by swift packet, and the
river was alive with boats, many of them carrying
produce to market – and manure from the town
back to the farmers on its banks.

There was another side to life on the Irwell.
Rowing was a popular activity on the river, and

there were rowing clubs holding regular regattas.
One of the owners of pleasure and racing boats,
and a former ship carpenter for the Old Quay
Company, was Mark Addy, senior, father of a
famous local hero. His son, also Mark Addy,
born in 1838 was a celebrated swimmer and oars-
man. He began his exploits at an early age:

Mr I. Lythgoe . . . got entangled in the
crowd of boats afloat, and so capsized.
Young Mark, then seven years old,

Four-Oar
(Badminton Library, *Boating*)

A Boat Accident – Rescued
(Badminton Library, *Swimming*)

called his father to the rescue of the sculler, and so perhaps commenced the long series of rescues, totalling over fifty lives, which are recorded to his honour. He managed to save two lives before he learnt to swim, one by wading into the water, and one by floating astride of a plank. He soon learnt to swim at the Greengate Baths, one of several large establishments of baths and wash-houses provided by a philanthropic company, long before the Corporations provided such places at the public cost.

(*The River Irwell*)

Mark Addy died 9 June 1890 from consumption. His death was said to have been hastened by the rescue of a child from the Irwell, where a sewer and poisonous gases made the river extremely toxic.

To see the joy of his brother and sister when I brought him out, to feel their grip round my legs, and hear them thank me a hundred times, was more to me than all else besides . . .

(Badminton Library, *Swimming*)

A fund was raised in his memory which provided annual prizes for swimming at the Salford Public Baths. The fund also erected an obelisk over his grave at Weaste cemetery, and donated a picture to the Peel Park Picture Gallery.

Another unlikely activity, given the state of the river, was fishing. *Anglers' Evenings*, published in 1880, records memories of members of the Manchester Anglers Association. The extract below is from 'Angling in the Irwell; a record of memories and hopes' by Edward Corbett:

. . . old traditions of some ten and twenty years then gone, told of good fishing in the Irwell. We heard of the time when fine salmon were caught opposite the New Bailey.

About the year 1819 I have, from the New Bailey Bridge (now called Albert Bridge), watched the fish on the shoals at the lower sides of the piers, and seen innumerable fish both there and at the

An Albert Medal. The Albert Medal, First Class, was awarded to Mark Addy by Queen Victoria in recognition if his gallantry and daring. The medal was presented to him on 14 January 1879 at Salford Town Hall by the Mayor
(Badmington Library, *Swimming*)

packet station near the old Barracks (then opposite the New Bailey). These were chiefly gudgeon; but other fish were seen rising to flies – and so numerous were the flies that the air was lively with swallows and house-martins; and the 'Old Quay boys' used to stand on the bridge and whip them down, with a long, heavy, short-handled whip, adroitly throwing the lash so as to kill the poor birds. It was a favourite amusement for us to count the swallows' nests along the Salford Crescent,

Illustration from title page
(Badminton Library, *Fishing*)

Frontispiece, *Anglers' Evenings*

and there were two or more in every window of the cotton mill at the river side opposite the New Bailey. There are no nests there now to be counted.

What had been the main artery of the town had become, by the end of the century, like a diseased heart clogged with silt and filth as industry continued to discharge waste into its waters.

*Once upon a time, were you inclined your weary limbs to lave, sir,*
*In summers's scorching heat, in the Irwell's cooling wave, sir,*
*You had only to go to the Old Church for the shore, sir;*
*But since those days the fish have died, and now they are no more, sir.*

(Grindon, *Lancashire*)

# CHAPTER 4

# 'A Very Fine Parish Church'

## *The Cathedral and Chetham's*

[A] respectable personage was gazing stead-fastly at the Old-Church Clock, over the battlements of the bridge. He had his own watch in his hand of ample size and antique appearance; and I saw that he was going to regulate its time by that of the venerable old time-teller in the tower of the Collegiate Church. Knowing that at that moment the Old-Church Clock was not, as they say, 'quite right', I could not resist the inclination to caution.

'My friend,' said I (taking out my own watch at the same time, to give some force to my words), 'that clock is six minutes too slow.'

'It may be so, sir,' said he, looking at me, viz., as an old acquaintance, 'it may be so; but I always set my watch by that clock, every week, whether it be right or wrong!'

'Indeed,' I exclaimed; 'that seems a strange fancy.'

'It may be so,' said he, 'and perhaps it is. But, sir, I know that clock of old; five and forty years I have gone by it, and it has never led me far wrong yet . . . It is

'It may be so, sir, it may be so, but I always set my watch by that clock, every week, whether it be right or wrong!'
(*The Old Church Clock*)

View of Victoria Bridge, Manchester
(Chethams, Assheton Tonge Collection)

now the oldest friend I have in Manchester, and I keep up my acquaintance with it by setting my watch by it every Saturday.'

(Parkinson, *The Old Church Clock*)

Few may now set their watches by the 'Old Church Clock', but the Collegiate Church is still one of the 'oldest friends' many have in Manchester. It has been the centre piece of the town since the fifteenth century.

James Hunnewell, surveying England's cathedrals in 1886, had mixed views of the old church in Manchester:

In this very large and busy city, veiled in its smoke, close by the even busier railway station, stands one of the least ancient minor English cathedrals, styled in Murray 'a very fine parish church'. If in size and general design it does suggest one, it can, with fairness, be called a superb example. Originally collegiate, built wholly since the fifteenth century began, and recently restored or decorated, it was as late as

1848 made the cathedral of the great See of Lancashire.

(*England's Chronicle in Stone*)

Although the building itself was not 'ancient', there was evidence of a church on the spot before Norman times:

We have evidence from the Domesday Book (1080–1086) that an ecclesiastical establishment existed in Manchester at least so far back as the reign of Edward the Confessor. The following quotation informs us that in the time of 'King Edward the Confessor, the church of Saint Mary and the church of St Michael held in Manchester one carve of land free from all customs save (Dane) geld'. These two churches probably held their lands jointly, and together formed one rectory and Parish Church of Manchester . . .

As regards this old church, and in fact anything previous to 1422, very little is known. As stated in the Collectanea of

Misereres. 'A fox with a goose on its back, running away from a woman – a child tries to pull the woman back into the cottage. In the left circle is an old fox in a sitting posture, with a birch rod over his shoulder, teaching two young cubs to read; in the right one is another old fox also sitting, holding a book between his fore-legs, in which he is apparently reading.'
(Worthington, *An historical account . . .*)

Manchester, probably from 627 to 1066, the church was of wood, but afterwards replaced by a stone structure. Some authorities state it to have been a timbered building, somewhat similar to the chapel of Denton near Manchester. Hollingworth tells us that one part of the wooden building was removed to 'Oardsall', and another part to Clayton, but most to Trafford, which in 1656 was known as 'the greate barne'.

(Worthington, *Historical Account*)

The present cathedral dates back to the fifteenth century, owing its collegiate endowment to Thomas de la Ware who, according to Thomas Fuller, had self-interested motives for his benevolence:

The Pope allowed him to marry for the continuance of so honourable a Family, upon condition that he would build a Colledge for such a number of Priests (Fellows under a Warden) as the Bishops of Durham and Lichfield should think fit; which he did accordingly, in Manchester. The Endowment of this *Collegiate* and *Parochiall Church* were the Gleab and Tithes of the Parsonage of that parish; and besides them, scarce any other considerable Revenue.

(*Worthies of England*)

Whatever the truth of this rumour, there is no doubt that a new church was needed as the old was no longer adequate nor suitable for the increasing size and prosperity of the town:

the pious De la Warre, who possessed the patronage of the living of Manchester, [decided] to attempt the foundation of a new and capacious church commensurate with the increased extent of the town, as well as of a suite of buildings capable of accommodating the additional number of clergy who would be required for the administration of its sacred rites. Yet the tongue of slander was not wanting – ready to impugn the generous intention of the donor, and to assign to it a sinister motive. Although he was upwards of sixty years of age, it was alleged that the design he entertained of founding and endowing a college was a condition upon which the pope acceded to a solicitation he had made to remove from him the restriction under which, as a priest, he laboured, and to allow him, in consideration of his being the last male branch of his family, to take unto himself a wife.

(Hibbert, *History of the College*)

The gothic church survived the centuries with difficulty. Partly because of lack of funds and partly through neglect, by 1635 it had fallen into

Cathedral, Manchester
(Chethams, Assheton Tonge Collection)

disrepair. Parishioners petitioned the King, complaining:

> And furthermore, so great danger from the church itself, that was ready to fall, did hang over the heads of them that entered thereinto, that many parishioners durst hardly fetch thence the spiritual food of their souls for the danger of their bodies, whereupon the fellows, being destitute of necessaries for their living, did also fear that the people would be shortly destitute of the eldership itself, except we would vouchsafe abundant grace, which they did most humbly beseech, to afford remedy to so many and so great evils.
>
> (*History of the College*)

Despite this, and further centuries of neglect, decay and repair, it was still a notable sight when visited by Hugh Miller in 1847, although by then the industrial climate was beginning to have its dire effect:

Externally the Collegiate Church is sorely wasted and much blackened; and, save at some little distance, its light and elegant proportions fail to tell. The sooty atmosphere of the place has imparted to it its own dingy hue; while the soft New Red Sandstone of which it is built has resigned all the nicer tracery entrusted to its keeping, to the slow wear of the four centuries which have elapsed since the erection of the edifice.

> (*First Impressions*)

It was not only the ravages of time and Manchester soot which damaged the Cathedral. Well meaning 'improvements' could be equally devastating. During the extensive renovations carried out towards the end of the nineteenth century there was much criticism of earlier attempts at preservation:

> the greatest havoc was wrought in the interior early in the present century under a pretext of improvement, when the beautiful columns and arches of the nave, the superincumbent clerestory, the great choir

34

Cathedral, Manchester, Nave
(Everett, *Manchester Guide*)

Interior of Collegiate Church, Manchester
(Chethams, Langton Scrapbook)

arch, the piers and arches of the outer north aisle or Trinity chapel, and the tower arch and wall above it, were hacked over with a pointed pick, and then coated with cement three-quarters of an inch in thickness. As an inevitable consequence, the mouldings and architecture were ruined and thrown out of all proportion, and the stability of the structure itself seriously imperilled . . . Nor did the masonry only suffer, for the ancient roof of the inner aisles of the nave, elaborately moulded, and having richly carved bosses at the intersections of their timbers, were hacked in a like manner . . .

(Crowther, *Architectural History*)

Yet, whatever the structural problems of the Collegiate Church, it did provide the focus for the spiritual life of the town. The extent of this was reported by Sir George Head in a visit earlier in the century:

I attended the Old Church . . . in order to witness the solemnization of several marriages. . . . I had heard on the preceding

Sunday the banns proclaimed as follows: – For the first time of asking, sixty-five; for the second time, seventy-two; for the third time, sixty.

(*A Home Tour*)

Head was present at a relatively small ceremony – only twelve couples:

The clerk, who was an adept in his business, and performed the duties of his office in a mode admirably calculated to set the people at their ease, and direct the proceedings, now called upon the [couples] to arrange themselves altogether round the altar. In appointing them to their proper places, he addressed each in an intonation of voice particularly soft and soothing, and which carried with it the more of encouragement as he made use of no appellative but the Christian name of the person spoken to. Thus he proceeded: 'Daniel and Phoebe; this way, Daniel; take off your gloves, Daniel. – William and Anne; no, Anne; here, Anne; t'other side, William. – John and Mary; here, John; oh, John; gently, John.'

35

Dr Dee
(Croston, *Nooks and Corners*)
'The appointment of Doctor Dee to the Warden-
ship was an act which cannot be justified. Dee was
frequently absent from his charge, and entirely abandoned it during the closing years of his life.'
(*The Palatine Notebook*)

and then addressing them all together:
'Now all of you give your hats to some
person to hold.' Although the
marriage-service was generally addressed to
the whole party, the clergyman was scrupu-
lously exact in obtaining the accurate
responses from each individual.

A previous incumbent was far less assiduous in
his duties – probably the most famous to hold
the office of warden: Dr John Dee.

Dee's church principles were not particularly pronounced. Devoted to

mathematical and scientific pursuits, he did
not greatly concern himself with either
Popish or Puritan theology; preaching was
not in his line, and he cared little for
those controversial sermons which only
provoked strife between the professors of
the old and the new faith, and excited bit-
terness in the minds of all.

(Croston, *Nooks and corners*)

Dee was appointed in 1596 amid 'great pomp
and solemnity', but:

At Manchester he had to deal with a rude,
boisterous, and uncultivated people, who
openly reviled him – a rough metal that all
his incantations and alchemical skill could
not transform into refined gold; and withal
he had to contend with a body of clergy
who abhorred the unlawful arts he was supposed to practice, and who treated him in
consequence with implacable hatred. Of a
truth his position was not an enviable one.

(*Nooks and corners*)

Dee's own diary attests to the difficulties he
encountered, but also shows the little weight he
gave to them:

Sept. 11 [1600] Mr Holland of Denton, Mr
Gerard of Stopford, Mr Langley &c., Commissioners from the bishop of Chester auth-
orized by the bishop of Chester did call
me before them in the Church abowt thre
of the clok after none [noon], and did deliver to me certayn petitions put up by the
fellows against me to answer before the
18th of this month. I answered them all
*eodem tempore* [at once], and yet they gave
me leave to write at leiser. Circa 7 a
meridie a storme of hayle and a clap of
thunder with some lyghtening.

(*Local Gleanings*)

Dr Dee survived this and other criticisms from
his fellow clerics. More dangerous were the
rumours of his dabbling in black magic:

Accordingly Dr Dee was formally accused
of practising witchcraft, and a petition
from him dated 5th January 1604 . . . sufficiently indicates the horror excited by

Humphrey Chetham Esq.
(Whatton, *A History of the Chetham Hospital*)

the charge. 'It has been affirmed that your Majesty's supplicant was the conjurer belonging to the most honourable privy council of your Majesty's predecessor of famous memory, Queen Elizabeth, and that he is, or hath been, a caller or invocater of devils or damned spirits. These slanders, which have tended to his utter undoing, can no longer be endured; and if, on trial, he is found guilty of the offence imputed to him, he offers himself willingly to the punishment of death, yea, either to be stoned to death, or to be buried quick, or to be burned unmercifully.'

(Harland, *Lancashire Folk-Lore*)

Fortunately Dee was never put to the test, but he was only to survive four more years, dying in abject poverty.

A less notorious, but equally significant, seventeenth-century figure connected with the collegiate institute was Humphrey Chetham. By mid-century both church and college were falling into disrepair. The Civil War brought the college buildings into the hands of sequestrators:

The building and outhousing fell into decay, and became ruinous; and there is little doubt this interesting relic would have disappeared altogether but for the timely interposition of one of Manchester's most worthy sons. Humphrey Chetham, a

wealthy trader, who had amassed a considerable fortune, conceived the idea of founding an hospital for the maintenance and education of poor boys, and also the establishing of a public library in his native town. He entered into negotiations with the sequestrators for the purchase of the College . . . in his will Chetham directed that his executors should make the purchase, if it could be accomplished. After his death this was done, the building was repaired, and from that time to the present, a period of more than two hundred years, it has continued to be occupied in accordance with the founder's benevolent intention.

(Croston, *Nooks and corners*)

The survival of the buildings provided an opportunity for one of those romantic flourishes so appealing to nineteenth-century writers:

Of those who make up the mighty tide of human life that daily sweeps along the great highway of traffic between the Manchester Exchange and the Victoria railway

Chetham College, 1828
(Chethams, Assheton Tonge Collection)

Chetham's Scholars
(Whatton, *A History of the Chetham Hospital*)

Station, how few there are who ever give even a passing thought to the quaint medaeval relic that stands within a few yards of them almost the only relic of bygone days that Manchester now possesses – the College. Pass through the arched portal into the great quadrangle, the College Yard as it is called, and what a striking contrast is presented. Without, all is noise and hurry and bustle; within, quietude and seclusion prevail. The old place is almost the only link that connects the Manchester of the present with the Manchester of yore; and surely it is something to feel that within this eager, striving, money-getting Babylon there is a little Zoar where you may escape from the turmoil, and the whirl, and the worry of the busy city, and, forgetting your own chronology, allow the memory to wander along the dim grass-grown aisles of antiquity, recalling the scenes and episodes and half-forgotten incidents that illustrate the changes society has undergone, and show how the past may be made a guide for the present and the future.

Humphrey Chetham's Coat of Arms
(Chethams, Manchester Scrapbook)

It was not just the College which attracted admiration, but the scholars themselves in their distinctive dress:

When the writer first attended service in this church [the Cathedral], on a Sunday, an attractive part of the large congregation was a group of children from one of those English institutions well recalled by the name of Chetham. The girls were dressed in blue set off by long white aprons, and the boys in long blue surtouts with silvery buttons.

(Hunnewell, *England's chronicle*)

But it is the German, Kohl, who must have the last word and draw the moral from 'worthy Humphrey Chetham' and his benefaction:

The scholars are the children of poor but respectable parents, and must all be brought up to some particular handicraft. When we consider what a noble renown the old worthy has earned for himself by this foundation, what benefits he has conferred, and still will confer, upon future generations, and what blessings have glorified his memory for two hundred years, we cannot help wondering how the wealthy can ever resist the temptation of thus building up for themselves an immortal monument in the gratitude and reverence of posterity. Many might do so at little or no sacrifice. If among every hundred or every thousand inhabitants of Manchester, who attained great wealth, only one were to think and act like old Humphrey Chetham, the whole land would be crowded with similar beneficent institutions. But these people seem all to carry in their hearts the precept which old Chetham only bore on his coat of arms: 'Quod tuum, tene!'

(*Ireland, Scotland and England*)

# CHAPTER 5

# 'The Ever to be Honoured Town'

## Civil War

The ever to be honoured town of Manchester in Lancashire, the Garrison thereof being but few in number, and brought to great penury, yet most gallantly issued forth, beat the Lord Strange, raised the siege, and took many prisoners.'

(Ricraft, *A Survey of Englands Champions*)

In July 1642 a 'linen webster,' Richard Parcival, was shot during a scuffle in Manchester – it is claimed that he was the first fatality of the Civil War.

The skirmish took place during a visit of Lord Strange (heir to the Earl of Derby) to fellow Royalists in the town. During dinner he was warned that Mr Holcroft, a Parliamentarian, was:

. . . marching in the towne with souldiers armed with pikes and muskets, with their matches lighted and cockt, also a drum beating before him to assemble more companie (their muskets also were charged with bullets, as appeared by those which were taken from them) who presented themselves in the street in a warlike posture . . .

(*Civil War Tracts*)

In the ensuing mêlée Lord Strange was fired on

Mounted Musketeer
(Fairholt, *Costume in England*)

Pikeman and Musketeer from a print dated 1645
(Fairholt, *Costume in England*)

'On 26th September . . . Houses were damaged and the attackers almost effected an entry into Deansgate. This was repulsed by twenty musketeers dispatched by Rosworm.'
(Frangopolu, *Rich Inheritance*)

and Parcival killed. An eyewitness wrote: 'What the issue will be, God best knows'. The issue was the siege of Manchester.

By September, King and Parliament had taken up arms in earnest and rumours reached Manchester that the King's supporters were pillaging Cheshire. The population around the town were so alarmed that they marched for safety to join the militia and townspeople. On the 24th Lord Strange led his troops from Warrington to bring the unfortified town to heel. The inhabitants refused to submit:

> But the Townsmen having some notice on the Saturday Evening of their approach, did send to the Inhabitants thereabouts, who on Sunday and MONDAY came in abundantly with Muskets, Pikes, Halberts, Staves, and such like, to the number of two thousand . . .
>
> And upon SUNDAY forenoone we were called out of Church from Sermon, and since then there have been many hot skirmishes both in the Night and Day, especially MONDAY in the afternoone and in the night, their Ordinance killed none, but onely a strange boy was gazing about him, but not in armes.

> (*Civil War Tracts*)

The town was unfortified. Fortunately help was at hand in the form of a German engineer, Colonel Rosworm, a veteran of the Thirty Years War. Hearing that conflict was likely in England, he had come to offer his experience to whoever would pay for it. His first offer was to the town of Manchester. He would superintend the defence for the sum of thirty pounds – thirty gentlemen covenanted to pay him! A counter-offer from Lord Derby of £150 was refused.

> But £30, if backed by my promise, contract, or engagement, I have learned to value above all offers, honesty being worth more than gold.

> (Whatton, *History of the Collegiate Church*)

By 23 September Colonel Rosworm had completed the defences:

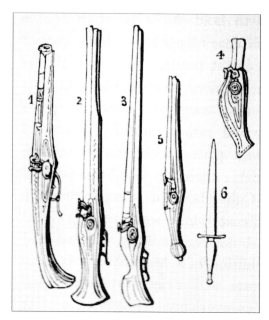

A group of arms. Seventeenth-century weapons:
1. A Dragon; 2. A wheel lock cavalier; 3. A wheel lock petronel; 4. Pocket wheel lock dog; 5. Wheel lock pistol; 6. Bayonet.
(Fairholt, *Costume in England*)

> We have been full of feares, often called out of Bed in the night and in great distresse, but Gods great goodness hath greatly preserved us beyond all expectation, If I would but related unto you all the passages it would fill you with admiration, to see how gratious God hath beene to use, but the town is better for some fortifications made by a GERMAN by Chains and Mudwalls at the Townes ends . . .

> (*Civil War Tracts*)

The nature of the fortifications was imaginatively re-created by Ainsworth:

> Commencing on the left bank of the Irwell on the south-west, these fortifications passed Deansgate, at the further extremity of which there was a barricade, enclosed the whole of Acres Field, and Pool Fold, where Radcliffe Hall was situated, passed on to the upper end of Market-street Lane, and skirting the fields between that thoroughfare and Shude Hill, terminated

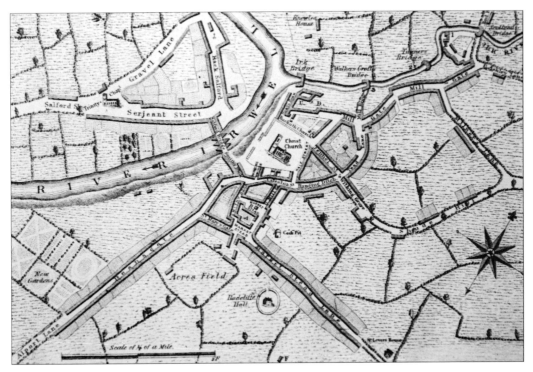

A Plan of Manchester and Salford taken about 1650, ed. John Harland
(Court Leet Records of Manchester)

Old Church and Bridge from Blackfriars
(Corbett, *The River Irwell*)
'Those forces which were in Salford endeavoured in the afternoon to enter the bridge, where they found
such hot entertainment . . . they were forced to retreat.'
(Whatton, *History of the Collegiate*)

at the bottom of Mill Lane . . . In Acres
Field and at no great distance from Radcliffe Hall – a picturesque old mansion,
occupied by Captain Richard Radcliffe –
a mount had been reared, whereon two
small pieces of cannon were planted.
Here, also, was a large building in which
the troops composing the garrison here
quartered, and where the magazine was
kept.

(*The Leaguer of Lathom*)

On Tuesday, 27 September, Lord Strange called
on the town to surrender – 'Not so much as a
rusty dagger' was the reply.

After a struggle of some days the besiegers
quit the attempt, with the loss of 200
men, the besieged having lost only four
killed and four wounded. The houses,
however, were much damaged, and
plunder to the amount of £10,000 was
said to have been carried away by the
Royalists . . . The decided adherence of
the people of Manchester to the parliamentary side caused it to be said – 'That had
not this town stood firmly to the king
and parliament, the whole country would
have been brought into subjection to the
oppression and violence of the cavaliers'.

(*Manchester Historical Recorder*)

The man largely responsible for this, John Rosworm, found that gratitude was short-lived once
the emergency had passed. In 1649 and again in
1651 he was petitioning for back pay:

. . . did I hazard my life, limbs, and all
that was dear to me, and do the richest of
you grudge me a few shillings by the
yeer, to buy me and mine food: is this
your equitie? . . . would you, indeed,
murder me, my wife and children after
the highest manner of cruelty, that under
God have been a means of preserving you
alive? What! is no other death fit for me
but famishing?

(*Civil War Tracts*)

Parliament found in his favour – but there is no
evidence in the Manchester account books that

Colonel Rosworm (spelt variously Rosworm,
Roseworm, Rosworme)
(Chethams, Langton Scrapbook)
'the complete soldier of fortune, [that] he never
inquired into the merit of the cause for which he
fought.'
(Whatton, *History of the Collegiate*)

the debt was finally paid. Manchester became
the Parliamentary headquarters for Lancashire.
Salford remained loyal to the King throughout.

On 23 April 1661 Manchester celebrated the
restoration of the monarchy. Captain Mosley
marched from Ancoats Hall with a company of
two hundred men, some of whom had fought
with him for the King in 1642. After a service
at the Old Church there was a 'grand procession'
through the town to the conduit and its 'three
streams of claret'.

The most Excellent Sir Thomas Fairfax, Captain
Generall of the Armyes etc.
(Ricraft, *A survey of England's Champions*)
'To illustrate this gallant Generals fame, were but to
light a candle against the sun . . .'

Ancoats Old Hall
(Chethams, Manchester Scrapbook)

It was nearly a hundred years later that Manchester was once again embroiled in a national upheaval.

*In the year Forty-four a Royal Visitor came*
*Tho' few knew the Prince, or his rank, or his*
*name*
*To sound the opinions, and gather the strength*
*Of the party of Stuart . . .*

(Quoted in Axon, *Lancashire Gleanings*)

There was a popular belief that Bonnie Prince Charlie, in disguise, visited Manchester in 1744 prior to the march from Scotland, staying at Ancoats Hall with Sir Oswald Moseley. Although there is no evidence for this the Jacobites undoubtedly anticipated a royal welcome when they arrived. They were to be disappointed:

Thursday 28th [November]: about three o'-clock to-day came into town two men in Highland dress, and a woman behind one of them with a drum on her knee, and for all the loyal work that our Presbyterians have made, they took possession of the town as one may say, for immediately after they were 'light they beat up for volunteers for P.C. [Prince Charles]'.

(Byrom, *Remains*)

There was no overt opposition but enthusiasm was lacking:

. . . although most of the leading inhabitants of the town were enthusiastic jacobites, their spirit had been more sparingly diffused among the middle and lower classes, with whom a strong bias in favour of the Pretender, by no means ardent enough to induce them to venture on the hazard stake of a chivalrous contest in defence of the antiquated doctrine of the divine right of kings. Accordingly, the Prince, upon entering Manchester, found that all the exertion which the town could make in his favour, was the formation of a regiment consisting of little more that three hundred men.

(Whatton, *History of the Collegiate Church*)

A sympathetic – and romantic – supporter, Beppy Byrom, reported in her diary:

Highland Chiefs.
(Logan, *The Scottish Gael*)
'the Manchester regiment was mustered in the church yard. On this occasion each officer appeared in a plaid waistcoat, with a white cockade, wearing also a sword by his side with a brace of pistols attached to his girdle . . .'
(Whatton, *History of the Collegiate*)

Charles Edward Stuart.
(Johnstone, *Memoirs of the Rebellion*)

'*When in Scottish costume, at the head of the clans,*
*He marched to Mancunium to perfect his plans,*
*The hope he had cherished from promises made*
*Remains to this day as a deb that's unpaid.*'
(Quoted in Axon, *Annals of Manchester*)

Saturday 30th: . . . then I dressed me up in my white gown and went up to my aunt Brearcliffe's and an officer called on us to go see the Prince, we went to Mr Fletcher's and saw him get ahorseback, and a noble sight it is, I would not have missed it for a great deal of money; his horse had stood an hour in the court without stirring, and as soon as he gat on he began a-dancing and capering as if he was proud of the burden, and when he rid out of the court he was received with as much joy and shouting almost as if he had been king without any dispute . . . [How delightful is the fair diarist's unsophisticated enthusiasm! If the Lancashire witches could have carried the day for Prince

Charles, his success would indeed have been certain – note by Parkinson.]
(Byrom, *Remains*)

The Lancashire witches did not have their way: the Jacobites were turned back at Derby and straggled back north finally to be defeated at Culloden. A number of Mancunians who had followed the Prince were executed for high treason on Kennington Common on 30 July 1716. One of these was 29-year-old Captain Dawson, the subject of a popular ballad:

> *Young Dawson was a gallant youth;*
> *A brighter never trod the plain;*
> *And well he lov'd one charming maid,*
> *And dearly was he lov'd again.*

45

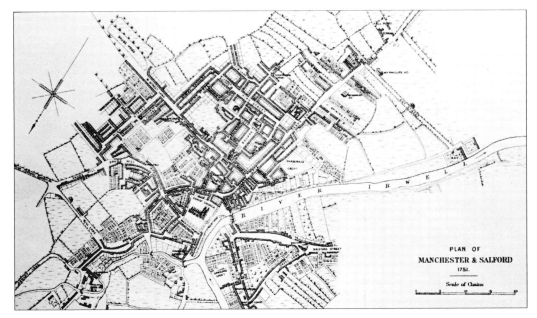

Plan of Manchester and Salford, 1775
(Shaw, *Manchester Old and New*)

*One tender maid she lov'd him dear*
*Of gentle blood the damsel came,*
*And faultless was her beauteous form,*
*And spotless was her virgin fame.*

*But curse on party's hateful strife,*
*That led the faithful youth astray,*
*The day the rebel clans appear'd:*
*O had he never seen that day!*

(Harland, *Ballads and Songs*)

The fate of his 'plighted fair one', Katherine Norton, was eminently tragic:

She got near enough to see all the dreadful preparations without betraying any extravagant emotions; she also succeeded in restraining her feelings during the progress of the bloody tragedy; but when all was over, and the shouts of the multitude rang in her ears, she drew her head back again

into the coach, and crying, 'My dear! I follow thee, I follow thee! Sweet Jesus, receive both our souls together!' fell upon the neck of her companion, and expired in the very moment she was speaking.

(Quoted in *Ballads and Songs*)

The heads of the traitors were sent to various towns as a warning to others. Two were sent to Manchester and displayed on the top of the Exchange.

The Constables' accounts of Manchester carry a (more) prosaic comment on the fate of these rebels:

Sept. 18 [1746]:
Expences tending the Sherriff this morn.
Syddall's and Deacon's heads put up,
1s. 6d.

(*Constables' Accounts*)

46

# CHAPTER 6

# 'A Triumph of Human Intelligence'

## Transport

It was more difficult then [1750] to reach a village twenty miles out of Manchester than it is to make the journey from thence to London now. [1861]

(Smiles, Lives of the engineers)

The difficulty lay in the state of the roads. Any journey in the eighteenth century was perilous, particularly so in Lancashire, as Arthur Young ruefully noted:

. . . let me most seriously caution all travellers who may accidentally purpose to travel this terrible country to avoid it as they would the devil, for a thousand to one but they break their necks or their limbs by overthrows or breaking down. They will here meet with ruts which I actually measured four feet deep, and floating with mud only from a wet summer. What must it be after a winter?

(Fishwick, Memorials of Old Manchester)

Yet Manchester's prosperity, depending as it did on trade, needed efficient transport. Conditions in the eighteenth century made even simple provisions difficult.

The imperfect state of the communications leading to and from Manchester

Barton Aqueduct
(Chethams, Langton Scrapbook)

Draught horse and barge on Barton Aqueduct
(Young, *A Six Months' Tour*)

The 'Red Rover'
(Chethams, Manchester Scrapbook)

rendered it a matter of some difficulty at certain seasons to provide food for so large a population. In winter, when the roads were closed, the place was in the condition of a beleaguered town . . .

(Smiles, *Lives of the Engineers*)

The solution lay in 'one of the greatest works of the age', conceived by the Duke of Bridgewater and James Brindley: a navigable waterway. The canal, which covered the seven miles from the Duke's colliery at Worsley to Manchester, halved the price of coal in the town and ushered in a revolution in water transport. By the end of the century the whole country was covered by a network of canals. Shortly after its opening, a correspondent to the *Annual Register* was full of enthusiasm:

Sir, Manchester Sept. 30
I have lately been viewing the artificial wonders of London, and the natural wonders of the Peak; but none of them gave me so much pleasure as the Duke of Bridgewater's navigation . . .
   At Barton-bridge he has erected a navigable canal in the air; for it is as high as the tops of the trees. Whilst I was surveying it with a mixture of wonder and delight . . . I durst hardly venture to walk, as I almost trembled to behold the large river Irwell underneath me, across which this navigation is carried by a bridge, which contains upon it the canal of water, with the barges in it, drawn by horses . . .

(*Annual Register*, 1763)

The horses, the non-human heroes of this revolution, were not altogether forgotten, as a later visitor to the museum of the Manchester Natural History Society testified:

Old Billy, for so he was named, worked all his life on the towing-path of one of the canals adjoining the city, and died on the 27th of November, 1822, at the wonderful age, testified beyond all manner of doubt, of sixty-two years. Before his demise he attained the honour of forming, decorated with ribands, part of a procession assembled at Manchester to celebrate the coronation of his Majesty King George the Fourth.
   Judging by appearances, Old Billy enjoyed perfect health to the last hour of his life. The head is well shaped, bearing the Norman character: the ears cropped, and the hair of the mane and foretop particularly fine, but bushy: besides the above preparation of the skin of the head stuffed, Old Billy's skull also occupies a place in the museum.

(Head, *A Home Tour*)

For the ordinary traveller horse-drawn transport was also a principal means of locomotion and this too began to improve:

The first coach from Manchester to London was not until 1754, when it was announced that the 'Flying Coach' would actually (barring accidents) arrive in London in four days and a half after leaving Manchester. Four years later the 'Flying Machine' was advertised to go from London to Liverpool in three days. In 1773 the Manchester and Liverpool stage-coach set out from the 'Spread Eagle' in Salford (in summer) on Monday, Wednesday, and Friday in every week and returned thither on Tuesday, Thursday, and Saturday.

(Procter, *Memorials of Old Manchester*)

Within the town as well wheels were turning:

In the year 1750, there was a stand of hackney-coaches in St Ann's square; but these vehicles being found less convenient for some purposes than sedan chairs, the latter took place of them, and few country towns have been better supplied with them. Some persons who had quitted trade began to indulge in the luxury of a chaise of their own to take an airing . . .

(Whitaker, *History*)

Later Swindells accounted for the failure of the hackney enterprise as 'the dwellers in the small town could easily walk to the outskirts in any direction'. As the town grew so did the need for more reliable, accessible transport. The hackney carriage service by 1824 had forty coaches

St Ann's Square, 1746
(Chethams, Manchester Scrapbook)

Hackney Coach

'Would you have me, said I, undergo the Punishment of a Coach again, when you Know I was so great a
Sufferer by the last, that it made my Bones rattle in my Skin, and has brought as many Pains about me, as if
troubled with the Rheumatism.'

(Clarke, *Social Life in the Reign of Queen Anne*)

in the town and its environs. Such transport became strictly regulated although, then as now, disputes might arise over fares:

Distances are to be computed from the Stand from whence the coach is taken, and to be measured the nearest Carriage-way. – In cases of dispute between Persons hiring a Coach and the Driver, as to the length of ground, the same shall be measured under the direction of a Justice of the Peace: and if the distance be greater than charged, the Persons refusing to pay shall be at all costs attending the

Carriages outside the Royal Institution.
Is the one on the right a "Bee"?
(Chethams, Assheton Tonge Collection)

admeasurement; if shorter, the Owner or Driver shall discharge the same.

(*Manchester Directory*)

Demand for transport became so great that the one-horse hackneys were supplemented by the forerunners of the omnibus:

> These have been described by several contemporaries . . . they must have been peculiar-looking machines, not over comfortable. They were square little boxes on wheels, holding eight or nine persons inside. At first they were styled 'The Bees'. At the front, in addition to the driver's seat, there was accommodation for three or four more passengers. The driver's position was not exactly a sinecure. In addition to managing his two horses, he had a horn which he blew at intervals in order to announce his progress. When a passenger wished to enter or leave the vehicle the driver alighted and opened the door, collecting the fares as the passengers alighted.

(Swindells, *Manchester Streets*)

Outside the town travel was still slow, inefficient and unreliable. Once again Manchester became the centre of a revolution in transport which soon transformed the entire country. The Liverpool and Manchester Railway was opened in 1830 after a competition for the best steam locomotive won by Stephenson's Rocket. Within a few years the line was returning a profit and a visiting French engineer waxed lyrical:

> . . . what a subject for admiration is such a triumph of human intelligence! What an imposing sight is a Locomotive Engine, moving without effort, with a train of 40 or 50 loaded carriages, each weighing more than ten thousand

The First Locomotive Engine built in Manchester
(Chethams, Langton Scrapbook)

| No. | Engines' Names. | Axle. | Size of Cylinder. | Situation of Cylinder. | Length of Stroke. | Makers' Names and Residence. | |
|---|---|---|---|---|---|---|---|
| | | | A LIST OF THE ENGINES USED BY THE COMPANY SINCE THE OPENING OF THE RAILWAY. | | | | |
| 1 | Rocket | Straight | 8 inch | Small Angle Outside. | 16 inch | R. Stephenson & Co. Newcastle. | |
| 2 | Meteor | do. | 10 | do. | do. | do. | do. |
| 3 | Comet | do. | 10 | do. | do. | do. | do. |
| 4 | Arrow | do. | 10 | do. | do. | do. | do. |
| 5 | Dart | do. | 10 | do. | do. | do. | do. |
| 6 | Phœnix | do. | 11 | do. | do. | do. | do. |
| 7 | North Star | do. | 11 | do. | do. | do. | do. |
| 8 | Northumbrian | do. | 11 | do. | do. | do. | do. |
| 9 | Planet | Double Crank | 11 | Under Boiler, Horizontal. | do. | do. | do. |
| 10 | Majestic | Straight | 11 | Small Angle Outside. | do. | do. | do. |
| 11 | Mercury | Double Crank | 11 | Under Boiler, Horizontal. | do. | do. | do. |
| 12 | Mars | do. | 11 | do. | do. | do. | do. |
| 13 | Samson | do. | 14 | do. | do. | do. | do. |
| 14 | Jupiter | do. | 11 | do. | do. | do. | do. |
| 15 | Goliah | do. | 14 | do. | do. | do. | do. |
| 16 | Saturn | do. | 11 | do. | do. | do. | do. |
| 17 | Sun | do. | 11 | do. | do. | do. | do. |
| 18 | Venus | do. | 11 | do. | do. | do. | do. |
| 19 | Vulcan | do. | 11 | do. | do. | Fenton, Murray, & Co., Leeds. | |

List of Engines
(Everett, *Manchester Guide*)

pounds! What are henceforth the heaviest loads, with machines able to move such enormous weights? What are distances, with moters which daily travel 30 miles in an hour and a half? The ground disap-pears, in a manner, under your eyes; trees, houses, hills, are carried away from you with the rapidity of an arrow; and when you happen to cross another train travelling with the same velocity, it

Booking Office, Liverpool Road Station
(Chethams, Langton Scrapbook)

seems in one and the same moment to dawn, to approach, and to touch you; and scarcely have you seen it with dismay pass before your eyes, when already it is again become like a speck disappearing at the horizon.

On the other hand, how encouraging is the evident prosperity of those fine establishments. How satisfactory it is to acquire the proof that the Liverpool Railway produces 9 per cent interest . . .

(Pambour, *A practical treatise*)

Swindells, writing later, gave a more prosaic account of the day-to-day operation of the line:

When the Liverpool and Manchester Railway was opened in 1830, the Manchester terminus was the bottom of Liverpool Road. Passengers were booked much in the same way that they were under the stage coach system. The name of the passenger, the amount paid, and the destination were entered into a book, a counterfoil duly signed by the person booking the passenger being given the traveller. A waybill giving a list of the passengers was carried by the guard of the train. Armed with his slip of paper, the passenger was allowed to enter the station, but the slips were collected by the guard before the train started. The slips were only available for the particular train for which the passenger was booked . . . Very soon after the opening of the line, the Company took an office in Market Street at the corner of New Cannon Street, where passengers could be booked, and in order that they might arrive at Liverpool Road in time for the train, a series of omnibuses were run by the Company from Market Street to the station. First-class passengers were carried free, but second-class passengers were charged a small fare. Four omnibuses ran in all, and on them was painted in large characters the word 'Auxilium'.

(*Manchester streets*)

## SIGNALS.

**RED** is a Signal of **DANGER—STOP.**
**GREEN** „ CAUTION—PROCEED SLOWLY.
**WHITE** „ ALL RIGHT—GO ON.

These Signals will be made by **Flags** in the Daytime, and b
**Lamps** at Night.

In addition to this, any Signal, or the arm, **waved** violentl
denotes danger, and the necessity of stopping immediately.

### POLICE SIGNALS.

1. When the Line is clear, and nothing to
impede the progress of the Train, the Policeman on duty will stand erect, with his Flag
in hand, but show no signal, thus—

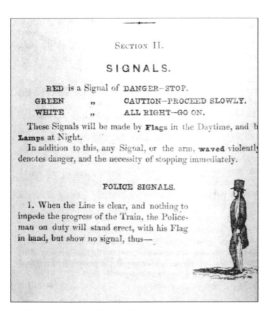

2. If it be necessary to proceed with
Caution, the Green Flag will be elevated,
thus :—

3. If it be necessary to proceed with
Caution from any defect in the rails, the
Green Flag will be depressed, thus :—

4. If required to stop, the **Red** Flag will be shown and
waved to and fro, the Policeman facing the Engine.

5. Engine-Drivers must invariably **stop** on seeing the Red
Signal.

6. As soon as the Engine passes, the Policeman will bring his
flag to the shoulder.

7. Every Policeman will be responsible for having his **Hand
Lamp** in good order and properly trimmed.

**STATIONARY SIGNALS.**

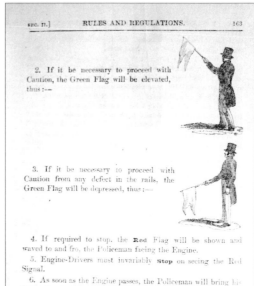

*Above and right*: Signals for use on the Manchester
and Liverpool Railway.
(*Rules and Regulations.*)

The new railway was not confined to passengers;
it became a formidable rival to the waterways
in carrying freight. Sir Thomas Head reported
from the loading bays of Liverpool in 1836:

> Among the various cargoes put on the car-
> riages with the greatest ease and despatch
> are pigs . . . This desirable object is ef-
> fected by means of a back entrance into a
> pig-yard, where all the herds that arrive,
> on their way to Manchester, find accom-
> modation. Hence there is a small door to
> a wooden platform, the latter leading, by
> an inclined plane, to the carriage standing
> on the railway, close to the mouth of the
> tunnel. The pigs enjoy this right of road
> unmolested, and in point of fact, step
> quietly out of their drawing-room into
> their vehicle, each as easily as an old dow-
> ager into her chair waiting in the vestibule.
>
> (*Home tour*)

Kohl confirmed that by 1844 railways had already established their importance for Manchester's trade:

> The enormous quantity of goods piled up
> in the warehouses of Manchester — the
> close vicinity in which the number of its

railways places it, to the woollen factories
of Leeds, the shawl and handkerchief
makers of Macclesfield, the silk weavers of
Coventry, the merino dealers of Bradford,
the light cotton wares of Preston, and the
heavy cotton goods of Halifax, &c., &c., –
the energy and rapidity of its steam-giant,
the universal servant of all work, which,
like Lord Chatham 'tramples on impossi-
bilities', – all the extraordinary means and
appliances which stand at the command of
its manufacturers and merchants, combined
with the industry, talent, and energy of
these merchants and manufacturers them-
selves- all these things contribute to
render Manchester beyond dispute the
manufacturing capital of the world.

> (*Ireland, Scotland and England*)

The 'servants' called upon to man so important
a service were under the strictest rule:

GENERAL REGULATION
APPLICABLE TO ALL SERVANTS
of the London and North-Western Company.

1. Each person is to devote himself exclusively to the Company's service, attending

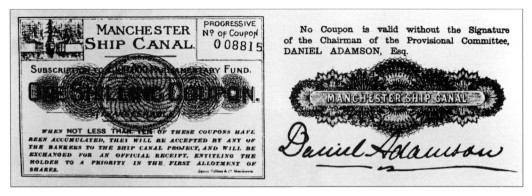

Manchester Ship Canal, 1/- coupon
(Tracy, *The Port of Manchester*)

during the regulated hours of the day, and residing wherever he may be required.

2. He is to obey promptly all instructions he may receive from persons placed in authority over him by the Directors, and conform to all the regulations of the Company.

3. He will be liable to immediate dismissal for disobedience of orders, negligence, misconduct, or incompetency.

4. No instance of intoxication on duty will ever be overlooked, and, besides being dismissed, the offender will be liable to be punished by a magistrate.

5. Any person using improper language, or cursing and swearing, while on duty, will be liable to dismissal.

6. No person is allowed to receive any gratuity from the public on pain of dismissal.

(*Rules and Regulations*)

The railways were not to have it all their own way. The ingenuity which had created the first inland waterway saw even greater opportunities in linking Manchester directly to the sea. As early as 1825 the *Liverpool Mercury* sounded a warning against such a proposal:

Humble Petition of the Liverpool Corporation to the Manchester Projectors of the Grand Ship Canal.

*Oh, ye Lords of the loom,*
*Pray avert our sad doom,*
*We humbly beseech on our knees;*
*We do not complain*
*That you Drink your champagne,*
*But leave us our port, if you please.*
*Sweet squires of the shuttle,*
*As ye guzzle and guttle,*
*Have some bowels for poor Liverpool!*
*Your great Ship Canal*
*Will produce a cabal,*
*Then stick to the jenny and mule.*
*Your sea scheme abandon*
*For rail-roads the land on:*
*And to save us from utter perdition,*
*Cut your throats if you like*
*But don't cut the dyke,*
*And this is our humble petition.*

(*History of the Manchester Ship Canal*)

Liverpool need not have worried – the scheme was shelved until 1883 and even when it was re-awakened there were doubters. The Mayor at the civic banquet welcoming the passing of the Ship Canal Bill rallied the feint-hearted:

If there be any man of wealth in our midst who will not come forward at this time to the help of those who have this project in hand, and will not do something beyond his own selfish interest and selfgratification, something in the interests of humanity (to use the words of Sir Walter Scott), he shall go down to the dust from which he sprung, unwept, unhonoured and unsung.

Mr Adamson [the promoter], in responding, paid a high compliment to his colleagues, the engineer, the solicitors, and the four counsel . . . and asked for the monetary support of the mercantile men of Manchester – of the support of the working classes he was already well assured.

(History of the Manchester Ship Canal)

Despite continuing financial problems the canal was opened in 1894:

Within three weeks of the opening the steamship *Venango* came up with a cargo of over 4,000 tons, and although the discharge of that vessel was to a large extent experimental and could be done now probably in a fifth of the time, the owners declared themselves well satisfied with the result.

On that proud occasion five months later (May 21st, 1894) when Her Majesty the Queen made a really genial royal

S.S. Pioneer: The Co-operative Society's Steamship 'the first cargo boat to enter the Manchester docks via the Ship Canal, and the first boat registered as belonging to the Port of Manchester.'
(Tracy, *The Port of Manchester*)

progress through Manchester to perform the ceremonial opening of the Canal, the pomp and circumstance attending the introduction to the docks of the Admiralty Yacht *Enchantress* and the two gunboats seemed almost humorous considering their size, and quite so considering the boom and the precautions observed. They were almost dwarfed by some of the passenger

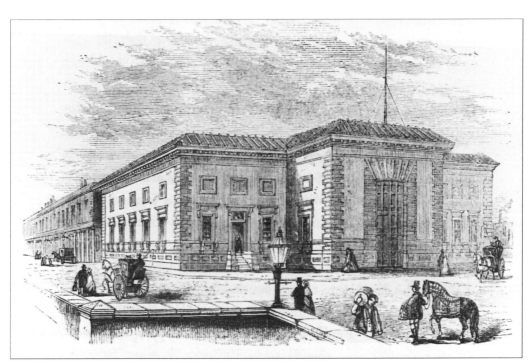

London Road Station
(Everett, *Manchester Guide*)

steamers that were carrying their thousands up and down.

(History of the Manchester Ship Canal)

However successful the Canal might claim to be, it could never rival the railway for romantic appeal. For the writer of fiction the railway carriage became a seductive centre for adventure and intrigue. Even prosaic London Road Station could, in the 1890s, be full of promise:

The platform of the London Road Station, Manchester, presented a busy scene of confusion and bustle, for the London express was timed to leave at 4.15. On this particular afternoon there seemed to be an unusual number of passengers, and the train was very crowded. Two gentlemen, however, who were comfortably ensconced in a first-class compartment near the engine, had managed so far to keep out intruders, a judicious tip to the guard having had a magical effect. Excited passengers had repeatedly rushed up to this compartment, but, finding the door locked, had growled out something naughty and gone to another carriage, much to the satisfaction of the two gentlemen . . .

At this moment the guard of the train hurriedly unlocked the door, and said apologetically, 'Gentlemen, I am sorry I cannot reserve the compartment for you, as the train is so full.' A porter came up carrying a hand-bag, a railway rug, bundle of umbrellas, and various odds and ends, and having deposited these things on the seat and in the rack, he got out and helped two ladies to get in. That done, the door was slammed to; the guard locked it; the shrill blast of the signal whistle resounded through the station; the engine uttered a shriek, and then the train went out into the fog on its way to London.

('Donovan', *The Man from Manchester*)

# CHAPTER 7

# 'A Manufacturing Town'

## The Cotton Trade

Cotton – *Gossypium Herbaceum.*
(*Vegetable Substances.*)
'the soft and beautiful vegetable substance forming
the covering or envelope of the seeds of the gossypium or cotton plant . . .'
(Quoted in Axon, *Annals of Manchester*)

*So may your Commerce stretch from Pole to Pole*
*Where'ere Suns shine, Winds blow, or Oceans*
*roll,*
*And may that Wealth with which your Trade is*
*crown'd*
*With every social Happiness abound.*

Mr Charles Lawson,
Manchester Grammar School, 1760
(Earwaker, *Local Gleanings*)

Before the advent of professional football, Manchester's most famous product was undoubtedly
cotton.

Manchester had been a clothing town from
the Middle Ages, though the Manchester cottons
or coatings were then a rough wool cloth prized
for its warmth and durability. A brief account
of the beginning of the manufacture of the
cotton we know today was given by Ellison in
1858:

The period of the introduction of the domestic manufacture of Cotton Wool into
Great Britain is generally stated to be
about 1585, in which year a number of
Belgian artizans, driven from their own
country by persecution, landed in Manchester. Queen Elizabeth received them
well, and encouraged the further immigra-
tion of their brother expatriots. Hence a
small work by Lewis Roberts, entitled the
'Treasure of Traffic', published in 1641,
states that Manchester had become distinguished for its Cotton manufactures, and
that the fustians produced there were
'then in almost general use throughout the
nation'.

(*A Hand-book of the Cotton Trade*)

Richard Guest, writing in 1823, thought that
the significant effects of the trade had not been
sufficiently recognised:

While admiration has been unboundedly
lavished on other triumphs of the mind,
the successive inventions and improvements of the Machinery employed in the
Cotton Manufacture, have obtained
neither the notice which their own
ingenuity, nor their national importance
required . . .
Under the influence of the manufacture

| VALUE. | 1821. | 1822. | 1823. | 1824. | 1825. |
|---|---|---|---|---|---|
| Exports to Ireland, | £7331 | £7595 | £5879 | £7234 | £6443 |
| twist & yarn, | 1,219,320lbs. | 2,120,515lbs. | 1,919,994lbs. | 2,360,786lbs. | 2,919,560lbs. |
| Imports from Do. | £1593 | £1324 | £2368 | £7768 | Not stated. |
| twist & yarn, | 27,551lbs. | 29,070lbs. | 46,972lbs. | 41,005lbs. | 124,268lbs. |
| ENTERED *per yd* | | | | | |
| Exports to Ireland, | 1,819,176 yds. | 2,827,285 yds. | 2,749,124 yds. | 3,392,924 yds. | 4,452,506 yds. |
| Imports from Do. | 516,717 yds. | 406,687 yds. | 556,046 yds. | 3,840,699 yds. | 6,418,645 yds. |

Cotton Wool Imported and Exported from 1781 to 1824
(Baines, *History and Directory*)

of which they have been promoters, the town of Manchester has, from an unimportant provincial town, become the second in extent and population in England . . . The origin of a Manufacturing town is this: a Manufactory is established, a number of labourers and artizans are collected – these have wants which must be supplied by the Corn Dealer, the Butcher, the Builder, the Shopkeeper – the latter when added to the Colony have themselves need of the Draper, the Grocer, &c. Fresh multitudes of every various trade and business, whether conducive to the wants or luxury of the inhabitants, are superadded, and thus is the Manufacturing town formed.

(*History of Cotton Manufacture*)

Such a 'Manufacturing town' was developing in Manchester in the early part of the nineteenth century. The new industry was jostling for space wih the old semi-rural market town:

When the Manchester trade began to extend, the chapmen used to keep gangs of pack horses, and accompany them to the principal towns with goods in packs which they opened and sold to shopkeepers, lodging what was unsold in small stores at the inns; . . . Soon after this period [1760] the vast increase of foreign trade caused many of the Manchester manufacturers to travel abroad; agents or partners were fixed in various cities on the continent, and Manchester at length

assumed in every respect the style and manners of one of the commercial capitals of Europe.

(Clarke, *The New Lancashire Gazeteer*)

This monopoly gave entrepreneurs the opportunity to exploit other commodities and other markets:

. . . the spinning of cotton is the principal branch of manufacturing carried on in Manchester, but a large proportion of the goods made in the other districts of the county are sold in this market, both for home and foreign consumption; and to such an extent has the commerce of this place attained, that foreigners have established agents, and sometimes have resident principals in this town, to conduct their commercial transactions.

(Baines, *History and Directory*)

By the time Kohl visited the town, the foreign presence was well marked:

I drove to Manchester in company with a German resident in that city. The number of Germans living in Manchester amounts, I believe, to somewhere about 1000.
There are in Manchester great numbers of foreign houses of business, which supply their own countrymen with the produce of this great manufacturing metropolis. Manchester and London are the only cities in England, where oriental mercantile houses are to be found.

(*Ireland, Scotland and England*)

The town's rapid expansion found the new

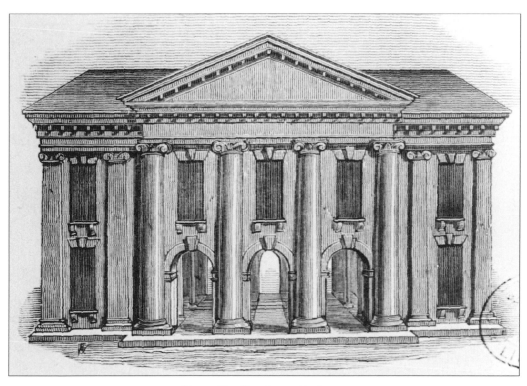

Above: The First Cotton Exchange
(Chethams, Manchester Scrapbook)
Below: The Exchange in 1850
(Ellison, *Manchester Handbook*)

Manchester, 1829
(Chethams, Assheton Tonge Collection)

jostling the old. Modern factories and palatial warehouses came to dominate the centre, driving the more prosperous residents to the outskirts.

Though the factory period . . . had begun so vigorously in Manchester, it still retained many of its primitive features and carried on its business within comparatively restricted limits. Its warehouses were to be found mainly in and about Cannon Street, a neighbourhood still retaining in its narrow courts and tortuous alleys many dingy survivals of that antique time, and where he who wanders there, may find much material for reflection in noting under what cramped and unlovely conditions these old manufacturers and merchants were content to do their business. Their residences were not far away from their warehouses, indeed often in close proximity to them, as some survivals of early domestic architecture, now devoted to trade uses, still testify.

(*Bannerman's Year Book*)

The firm of Bannerman and Sons was one of those pushing back the limits of the industrial and mercantile districts – and typical also of the attraction of the town to migrants, both capital and labour:

[The firm started in Market Sted Lane] Subsequently in 1817, a removal was made to Marsden Square, where the pioneer of the firm, David Bannerman, had first located himself, and whose experiences led to the migration hither of his father, Henry Bannerman, a Perthshire farmer, who brought along with him the rest of his sons, to establish the business inseparably connected with his name.

From there, according to Grindon:

They made what was considered a very bold advance, quite a new fashioned step indeed, changing their quarters to the top of Market Street, next door to the Royal Hotel. The rent while it was in Bannerman's hands was £500 per year;

Brunswick Mill, Ancoats, Manchester
(*Bannerman's Year Book*)

today [1877] about three fourths of the same premises fetch £1200.

(Quoted in *Bannermans*)

As might be expected the firm which was at the forefront of 'modernisation' built mills of high standard, as was reported to the Factory Commissioners in 1833:

A splendid work, erected only a few years ago, the site over walls 230 feet by 53. There is here an ascending and descending room, moved by steam; but what pleased me most, on going through the extensive apartments of this establishment, was to observe the sufficient space which each worker enjoys, so that even in an atmosphere generally heated to about seventy degrees there is at least apparently absent the effluvia created by any crowded number of human beings. There are about 74 workers in each of the spinning apartments, 225 ft long by 48½ wide: not more, relatively than are found in the drawing-room of persons assembled for a private dinner party. Dressing and undressing rooms are provided for female workers on each floor, in which their

working clothes are kept. There is also a pipe of spring water for drinking in each apartment, a large pipe of water for extinguishing fires in each storey, large fanners in the preparing room to free it from dust.

(Report by Mr Stuart)

However well built and modern the factory, there were still disadvantages. Kohl, touring Orell's Mill in 1844, found it of high standard, but still with faults:

[It] is a very complete factory; the cotton is brought to it raw from America or Egypt, and it is here cleaned, spun, and woven. It employs no less than 1300 looms. These are all placed in one great weaving room, in which 650 girls are constantly at work. The humming, beating, and whirring of all these looms filled the room with a noise like the roaring of the sea. The power-loom is said, not only to work ten times as fast as the hand-loom, but a great deal better; the woof is more smooth and even, because the stroke of the machine is more regular than that of the human hand . . .

The factory is one of the best built of

any; yet I found the air intolerably close and suffocating in some parts. I was also sorry to observe the terrible narrowness of the passes between the dangerous machines and their restless and gigantic arms and wheels; in these passes the floor was also extremely smooth and slippery.

(*Ireland, Scotland and England*)

The trade had also given rise to a well known Manchester character, the 'hooker-in'. These were men employed to attract buyers to view the stock, besieging inns every morning to accost the new arrivals. A Mr Thomas Brittain remembered them:

My connection with the Manchester trade from 1831 to 1845 brought me frequently in contact with the 'hookers-in', as they were familiarly called, and I knew many of them personally. They were known to each other pretty generally by nick-names . . . a Mr Lewis, was reported to have made an attempt on his own life; he was named Sudden Death ever afterwards. Previous to this one of the hookers-in had obtained the name of Murder – I cannot say why – and another the name of Battle; so that amongst this interesting fraternity there were 'Battle, Murder, and Sudden Death'.

The more successful of the hookers-in obtained excellent remuneration for their services. One of them was said to receive a thousand a year, and I am inclined to believe it. They were not a long lived race, for the daily discharge of their duties brought them into continual connection with the hotels, where they had to treat their clients . . .

(Slugg, *Reminiscences*)

By the end of the century the city was dominated by those temples to mammon: the warehouses. Imitating Italian palaces they were both impressive and efficient. *Bannermans Year Book* gives a guided tour of their establishment:

[It] is a massive brick building with a heavy stone cornice, and relieved in the frontages with courses of stone, but other-

Cotton Bales
(Chethams *Momus*)

Warehouse, 33 York Street
(*Bannerman's Year Book*)

wise unadorned. Passing through the plain stone doorway you find yourself in the close neighbourhood of ledgers, day books and the occupants of the counting-house, which is divided by the entrance and otherwise occupies the whole front of the building. Then you come upon a spacious vestibule, in which coloured glass is freely used for adornment, and where samples of cotton in process are shown . . . The warehouse is divided into sections and sub-divided into bays, lighted in the interior by glazed well spaces, and traversed by various avenues. In the basement, the area for goods is taken up by flannels, blankets, rugs, and oilcloths in racks and piles . . . [And so on through a further three or four storeys.]

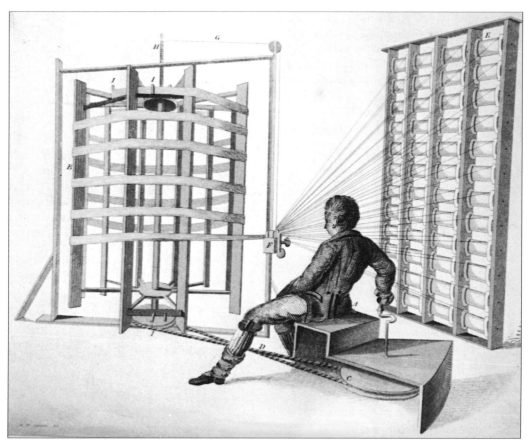

The Warping Mill
(Guest, *A Compendious History of the Cotton Manufacture*)

All this energy, industry and prosperity! Merchants luxuriating in their warehouses and offices went home to their mansions in Altrincham and Alderley Edge. Their workers were not so fortunate.

The first to suffer from the impact of industrialisation were the hand-loom weavers, once the aristocrats of the trade. Impoverished by competition with the new machinery, they were still desperately hanging on as late as 1841:

> It is astonishing how any of these can continue to earn a penny, in the unequal competition with the immense machinery and capital employed in the great factories. Yet it is an indisputable fact, that there still exist, in Manchester alone, no less than 3,192 hand-weavers. These work from morning till night, in close places,

with scanty nourishment and clothing, and suffering grievously from privation and want . . . I went through a number of their cellars, and I found many in which the loom was already at rest. Before one such, sat in unwilling idleness, the very image of silent despair, a poor half-starved weaver, who had not a penny to buy cotton, and who told me that he had been in vain seeking employment for eight days. On his table was a small plate of cold watery potatoes, saved from the scanty sustenance of the preceding day, to satisfy the hunger of the next.

(Kohl, *Ireland, Scotland and England*)

The old crafts were rapidly becoming defunct, the mills demanded a different kind of workforce and from the outset the employment of children aroused violent controversy. George Condy was one of the leaders of the Manchester campaign in favour of restricting child labour. He quoted, amongst many others, Dr T. Young, Physician, of Bolton:

> The first effects [of the long hours] appear to be upon the digestion; the appetite suffers, the digestion is impaired, and consequent emaciation and debility are induced. Scrofulous diseases are common.
>
> (*Argument . . . on Factory Children*)

Condy then later builds on the accumulated medical evidence:

> I spare the reader the recital of the description of varicose veins and their frequent consequence ulcerated legs – the almost invariably diseased lungs among adults who have spent their childhood in mills, especially in flax mills – the habitual disorder of the digestive organs – the perversion of the biliary secretions, which is assigned as the proximate cause of that sallow hue which distinguishes the factory population. I leave out the feebleness of the females . . . in the evolution of the foetus, the inevitable debility of the race so produced, and the consequence, in the estimation of philosophy so greatly to be desired, of its gradual extinction.

The first effective Factory Act restricting child labour was passed in 1833, but concern continued over conditions in general in the cotton mills. Kohl attributed the deficiencies of the factory system to the indifference of the master-manufacturers:

> The severity of discipline in the English factories, the cold, harsh manner in which the work people are addressed by their superiors, the rigid silence enforced among them, and the unfeeling manner with which they are dismissed to steal or starve, at every fluctuation in the fortunes of their masters, all these things cannot but have a hardening and deadening effect on their characters . . . It is commonly said in England that there is less personal inter-

'A little fellow sitting on a doorstep nursing a baby.'
(*Daddy's Bobby*)

course between the master cottonspinner and his workmen, than between the Duke of Wellington and the meanest cottager on his estate.

> (*Ireland, Scotland and England*)

Another eye-witness found the fault to lie largely with the workers themselves:

> Having had occasion to inquire into the peculiarities of the factory people of that town [Manchester], I recognised in their style of diet a very sufficient cause of gastralgia [irritability of the stomach] without laying blame on their mill avocations. Bacon enters very largely into their diet, and bacon of very indifferent quality, which I found on the most careful examination to be frequently rusty – that is, more or less advanced in the process of putrefaction . . . In the 'piquant' state, it suits vitiated palates accustomed to the fiery impressions of tobacco and gin.

A mill girl
(*Lass o'Lowries*)

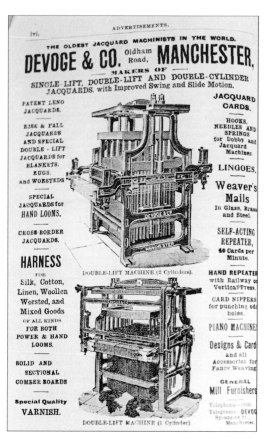

Devoge and Co., Manchester
(*Manchester Royal Exchange Directory*)

Mill Girls.
(Chethams *Momus*)

These three stimulants are too much used
by that order of work-people in Manchester who receive the highest wages . . .

(Ure, *Philosophy of Manufactures*)

Work in the factories, whatever the conditions,
was relatively well paid; and preferable to no
work at all. As the hand-loom weavers declined,
the cotton industry gave rise to a new and
vigorous group, distinct at the outset to Lancashire – the independent working girl:

> . . . a factory girl has more of the 'pro-
> fessional' about her than any class of men,
> excepting perhaps the soldier. The mill is
> her only possible [*sic*]. If she does not love
> its oily floors and noisy rooms, she has, at
> least, but very little idea of any other
> mode of life. She is introduced to the
> cotton factory at a very early age; from

morning till night she works in it, as girl, woman, and mother, till old age or good fortune interferes. The romance of her life, her friendships and her love are associated with the tall chimney, with the long rows of windows, and with her busy fellow-workers. She is one of a caste, and the suggestion to her of another mode of life is by no means welcome . . . The cherished independence of these girls, resulting from the demand for their labour, causes them to rely one upon another rather than upon their parents or relative . . .

(Arnold, *The Cotton Famine*)

The 'Manchester Examiner' reported a typical conversation between such working girls during the cotton famine of 1862:

Eh lasses! han yo bin a beggin' too? – Aye, lass, we han. Aw've just bin tellin' Ann here. Aw never did sich a thing i' my life afore – never! But it's th'first time and th'last for me – it is that! Aw'll go whoam, an' aw'll dee theer, afore aw'll go a-beggin' ony moor, – aw will for sure. mon it's sich a nasty, dirty job; aw'd soon clem! [starve] . . .

(Quoted in *The Cotton Famine*)

Such independent spirit was going to be needed in the future for the primacy of cotton which helped build Manchester's prosperity was not going to last much beyond the century. Fortunately the town had more to build on than the one industry. 'Cottonopolis' might die, but Manchester would prevail.

# CHAPTER 8

# 'Starving is Our Lot!'

## *The Poor*

The poor are always with us, but little recorded. Without the romantic fancies of earlier historians, it is difficult to reconstruct the lives of Manchester's poor.

Like the rest of the country the weakest of Manchester's population were prone to the ravages of disease and plague. They suffered terribly during the seventeenth century.

> Anno 1605. The Lord visited the towne (as 40 yeares before and 40 yeares after) wth a sore pestilence; there died about 1000 p[ersons], amongst wch Mr Kirk, chaplaine of the Colledge and his wife and foure children; all the time of the sicknesse Mr Burne preached in the towne so long as hee durst (by reason of the vnrulinesse of infected psons and want of gouetmt [government] and then hee went and preached in a feeld neere to Shooters brooke, the townespeople being on one syde him and the countrey people on another.
>
> (*Court Leet Records*)

The Burial register for the Collegiate Church shows that most of the deaths, 200 in July and August, were in the Summer months. In 1645, the 'Pestilence' was so great that the town was under quarantine. The town, honoured in 1642, became 'the only town untouched by the enemy, and the only town stricken by God'. An Order of Parliament was promulgated for a collection for the poor of Manchester:

> 9th December 1645
> Whereas the Towne of *Manchester*, in the County of *Lancaster*, one of the first towns in *England* that in this great cause stood for their just defence against the opposition and attempts of a very powerful army, hath for a long time been so sore visited with the Pestilence that for many moneths none were permitted either to go in or to come out of the said town . . . but many families like to perish for want, who cannot be sufficiently relieved by that miserably wasted countrey;

No. 230.—A Cripple.

Left: A cripple.  Right: A blind man and dog (from Wright, *The Homes of Other Days.*)
'The roads in the Middle Ages, appear to have been infested with beggars of all descriptions, many of whom were cripples, and persons mutilated in the most revolting manner.'

The Beggar and his Dog
(Bewick, *Select Fables*)

It is therefore ordered that there be a collection for the poor of the said town, in all the Churches and Chapels within the Cities of *London* and *Westminster*.

(*Civil War Tracts*)

As a growing centre of trade and industry Manchester suffered repeated visitations of contagious diseases, as grizzly evidence later showed:

Towards the end of the eighteenth century, on the occurrence of a great epidemic, several acres of land had been enclosed here [by the river Irk] for a supplementary cemetery, and after many hundreds of bodies had been interred, and the scourge had ceased its ravage the entrance to this was walled up. Then to all seeming the place was abandoned to the elements, and it became forgotten by men for at least a score of years . . . In the end, however, there came a year of great rains, and the high brick walls, burst out by the floods, carried with them in to the street below, much soil, the ends of many coffins, and a great number of human skulls, along with other gruesome relics of mortality.

(Redfern, *A City Idyll*)

Such natural disasters would strike the population indiscriminately; for the poor there was always concern and − often reluctant − efforts to assist. The Court Leet recorded attempts to create work:

5 October 1620
Whereas seuerall somes of money haue beene latelye given by dyuse [divers] Well disposed psons for the raisinge of a stocke and settinge to worke the poore of Manchestr . . .

(*Court Leet Records*)

In 1621 the first recorded charity for the poor was established under the will of Mr Edward Mayse:

7 May 1621
Item 1 I give and bequeath the sume of One hundred and twentie pounds to the vse of the Pore of Manchester to be bestowed and disposed of for the purchase of some lands Anuities or other profitts withall Convenient speed . . .

(*Court Leet Records*)

Lands were purchased in 1635 and the income funded the charity.

Whatever the efforts to help the poor, there were always the unscrupulous willing to exploit them, pursued here in the Court Leet:

7 May 1639
The Jurie of this Courte Leete findinge that the pore and other Inhabitants of this towne are Dailie abused by such psons as make breade of wheate & other graines, and sell to Inkeepers and others sixteene to the Dozen, and the people so buyinge sell the same for a peny a peece, to the great oppression of such poare and others as haue accation [occasion] to buy the same, order now that noe person what soeuer shall heareafter make or cause to bee made any breade of wheate or other graines of any smaler size or greater number then thirteene to the Dosin, *sub pena*★ for euery time offendinge vjs viijd [6s. 8d.]

(*Court Leet Records*)

★ *sub pena*: under penalty.

Such practices continued into the next century and beyond:

Upon presentment of the Officers Market Lookers for ffish and fflesh we do amerce James Green for offering for sale Beef not marketable two pounds two shillings.

Upon presentment of the Officers for tasting wholesome Ale and Beer we do amerce James Whittaker for selling Ale or Beer in Vessells both unsealed and short of Measure ffive Shillings.

Upon presentment of the Scavenger for Market place and Shambles we do amerce the following persons (Butchers) for not cleaning under their Stalls in the Old Shambles but suffering Rubbish and dirt to lye there to the great nusance of all the Inhabitants and Market-people in two Shillings and six pence each. [Twenty-nine offenders]

Easter 1743 (*Court Leet Records*)

Racketeers were not the only cause of high food prices; the geographic position itself was a contributing factor. The problems were outlined by Samuel Smiles:

. . . and even in summer, the land about Manchester being comparatively sterile, the place was badly supplied with fruit, vegetables, and potatoes, which, being brought from considerable distances slung across horses' backs, were so dear as to be beyond the reach of the mass of the population.

(*Lives of the Engineers*)

Assistance to the unemployed was centred on the Poor House, or paupers workhouse. Such a workhouse was built in 1792 at a cost of £30,000, on a site above the Irk and the Irwell opposite but beyond the Collegiate Church. Love gives the details:

The provision for the poor in Manchester is necessarily very extensive. The fluctuations in trade, together with the vast amount of Irish poor who flock to the town in search of employment, cause a heavy augmentation of the poor-rate. For the year ending March, 1839, upwards of £13,000 were distributed among the out-of-door poor, and in several departments about £1,600 more. The expenditure on the workhouse alone, during that period, was £8,751; of which sum £106 appears to be appropriated, with praiseworthy liberality, to tobacco and snuff for the more aged inmates, who, no doubt, consider these articles as essential to their comforts.

(*Manchester as it is*)

Workhouse
(Aston, *A Picture of Manchester*, 3rd edn)

The poor laws restricted the unemployed poor in receipt of relief to their own parish; loss of benefit resulted for all the family if the father went in search of work. This hindered the movement of labour as Manchester's mill owners complained to the Poor Law Commissioners. James Phillips Kay MD wrote:

Gentlemen, St Peters-square, Manchester, 22d July 1835
According to your instructions, I have been engaged, . . . in making inquiries, by which, perhaps, the Commissioners may judge how far it would be prudent to comply with the request of many of the manufacturers of the cotton districts of Lancashire and Cheshire, and furnish them with a supply of such well-disposed, honest, and industrious labourers from the South of England, as may hitherto have been restrained by the bondage of the late Poor Law from disposing of their own labour and that of their families in those districts where it would meet with the most ample rewards.

(*Report of the Commissioners*)

As the factories expanded and more and more people emigrated to the town in search of work, the labouring 'poor' became the subject of comment and investigation. 'Stricken by God' was no longer seen as the source of disease, the conditions in the city itself became the focus of concern.

James Kay in 1832 examined both the diet and the living conditions of Manchester workers:

. . . a sufficiency of animal food, wheaten-bread, and malt liquor, and as little liquid of other kinds as possible . . . *occasionally, though rarely,* a small sprinkling of bacon or other meat . . . The population . . . is crowded into one dense mass, in cottages separated by narrow unpaved, and almost pestilential streets; in an atmosphere banded with smoke . . . The operators are congregated in rooms and workshops during twelve hours in the day, in an enervating, heated atmosphere, which is frequently loaded with dust or filaments of cotton . . .

(*Moral and Physical Condition*)

Andrew Ure writing in 1835 commented on the food available – to all classes:

There is another thing which, as far as my experience goes is peculiar to Manchester. The most *respectable* bakers (exclusive of hucksters) occupy one side of their shops with cheese (sometimes also bacon) in every stage of decay, which never fails to impart its odour to the bread exposed to the effluvia. Certainly the savour of bakers' shops in London, Edinburgh, and Glasgow is far sweeter . . . I have noted this circumstance merely in confirmation of my statement with regard to the insalubrious dietary of the Manchester operatives.

Above: Soup Charity
(Chethams, *Manchester Mercury*, 23 February 1811)
Right: Advert for Patent Medicine
Chethams, *Manchester Mercury*, 13 September 1795)

The viands to be found upon the tables
of the middling and higher classes do not
yield in excellence of quality or culinary
refinement to those of any metropolis in
Europe.

(*The Philosophy of Manufacturers*)

The diet of the destitute amongst the population
became the concern of Richard Baron Howard,
physician to the Ardwick and Ancoats dispensary, formerly resident to the Manchester Poor
House. His study *An inquiry into the Morbid Effects
of Deficiency of Food . . .* (1839) pointed out the
effects of poor diet:

. . . it will be generally allowed that the
earnings of those employed in manufactures are adequate, with prudence and
economy, to provide a sufficiency of
wholesome food and clothing, and to pro-
cure all the necessaries of life. But these
classes are notoriously improvident: . . .
A large proportion even of those who
regularly receive high wages are constantly
in a state of the greatest poverty . . .
Their families are ill fed, scantily clothed
and badly lodged;

His description of his patients is graphic:

They are feeble and languid; their appetite
is often capricious and defective; their
nervous system alternately morbidly excited and depressed, whilst their muscular

and vascular systems evince a want of
tone and power . . . a large proportion of
the manufacturing classes is far from being
in a state of vigourous health and many of
them are on the verge of actual disease.

Drunkenness was a constant factor in reports on
the impoverished of Manchester:

From the indulgence in this habit [intem-
perance] many who regularly receive high
wages are constantly in a state of the ut-
most indigence — often bordering on
positive starvation . . .

Ure was equally censorious:

Hypochondriasis, from indulging in too
much the corrupt desires of the flesh and
the spirit, is in fact the prevalent disease
of the highest paid operatives, a disease
which may be aggravated by drugs, but
must seek its permanent cure in moral
regimen.

(*The Philosophy of Manufacturers*)

He had observed that workers were encouraged
to a degree of self-help by treating their complaints with an astonishing array of patent
medicines:

Nothing strikes the eye of a stranger more
in Manchester than the swarms of empiri-
cal medical practitioners of medicine.
Nearly a dozen of them may be found

clustered together in one of the main streets; all prepared with drastic pills and alternative potions to prey upon the incredulous spinners.

Kohl noted the practice by reading the placards on the walls of the town:

Here are the puffing announcements of quack-doctors, who recommend all kinds of life-pills, health-pills, and life-elixirs to the public, and who append divers 'Cautions to families', in which purchasers are warned to beware of various deleterious compounds, and requested to observe the superscription of the true medicine.

(*Ireland, Scotland and England*)

Howard's second report concentrated on living conditions and their effect upon health:

That the filthy and disgraceful state of many of the streets in those densely populated and neglected parts of the town where the indigent poor chiefly reside, cannot fail to exercise a most baleful influence on their health, is an inference which experience has fully found to be well founded; and no fact is better established than that a large proportion of the cases of fever which occur in Manchester originate in these situations . . . Many of the streets in which cases of fever are common are so deep in mire, or so full of hollows and heaps of refuse, that the vehicles used for conveying the patients to the House of Recovery often cannot be driven along them . . . In most of these places are to be seen privies in the most disgusting state of filth, open cesspools, obstructed drains, ditches full of stagnant water, dunghills, pigsties, &c. from which the most abominable odours are emitted.

(*On the prevalence of diseases*)

Howard's descriptions of 'open cesspools, ditches full of stagnant water, dunghills, pigsties, &c.' is reminiscent of sixteenth-century Manchester and the plague.

Commenting in 1808, Espriella (in reality the

'The five boxes of matches left over from the night before did to start with.'
('A Delver', *From Dark to Light*)

poet Robert Southey) contrasted the city with his native Spain:

The dwellings of labouring manufactures are in narrow streets and lanes, blocked up from light and air, not as in our country to exclude an insupportable sun, but crowded together because every inch of land is of such value, that room for light and air cannot be afforded them. Here in Manchester a great proportion of the poor live in cellars, damp and dark, where every kind of filth is suffered to accumulate, because no excertions of domestic care can ever make such homes decent. These places are so many hotbeds of infection; and the poor in large towns are rarely or never without an infectious fever among them, a plague of their own, which leaves the habitations of the rich, like a Goshen★ of cleanliness and comfort, unvisited.

(*Letters from England*)

★ See *Exodus* 10 v.23.

'and Tom, who had at last crawled back to die . . .
with a feeble and bitter groan of despair he sank
down on the frozen stones and knew nothing more.'
(Smith, *Pilgrim Street*)

The Night Refuge, St John's, Deansgate
(Tomlinson, *Bye-ways of Manchester Life*)

Outbreaks of fever had resulted in the opening of a temporary fever hospital in Balloon Street which Howard visited:

> I was much struck with the numbers who had suffered from want of food, clothing and shelter, previous to admission. Many had been long out of work, others followed no regular employment, and their means of support had been precarious and uncertain in the extreme; and some had passed several nights in privies or entries, from inability to procure lodging. A few had found temporary shelter in that excellent institution, the Night Asylum for the Destitute, established early in the year 1838, and which has indubitably saved many lives.

Kohl, too, commented on the starving poor:

> . . . there are a number of families in Manchester, whose members earn very high wages, and who, nevertheless, are living in a state of wretched destitution, bordering on starvation . . . There is probably no other country in the world where five shillings a week could not keep off starvation. Mr Love, also adds, from his own experience, that, numbers are yearly brought to a premature death from want of sufficient food . . .
>
> (*Ireland, Scotland and England*)

He also paid a visit to the Night Asylum and concluded after interviewing some of the residents that 'the greater number of the petitioners were artizans and mechanics'.

> 'I am a block-printer, sir, but in this stand-still of everything, I have had no employment for some months.'
> 'Cannot you find other employment? Can you do nothing else?'
> 'No, sir, I have been brought up for block-printing, and I have been a block-printer all my lifetime. I understand nothing else. Besides, the whole country is at a stand-still now. In my time I had a cow, and a little garden, which my wife attended to. My wife died last summer, and all the others things are gone away,

by the badness of the times.'
'Do not despair the times may mend.'
'Oh, no hope, sir! Starving is our lot! No
hope, sir!'

In a short piece written under the pseudonym,
'Cotton Mather Mills', Mrs Gaskell showed her
sympathy for Manchester's poor. As a visitor for
the Manchester Provident Society, she had first-
hand experience of the lives of Manchester's less
fortunate. The story, *Libby Marsh's Three Eras*,
confirms many of the observations made by Howard.:

> Mrs Dixon rattled out the tea things, and
> put the kettle on; . . . Then she called
> Anne down stairs and sent her off for this
> thing and that. Eggs to put to the cream,
> it was so thin. Ham to give a relish to the
> bread and butter. Some new bread (hot if
> she could get it). Libbie heard all these or-
> ders given at full pitch of Mrs Dixon's
> voice, and wondered at their extravagance,
> so different to the habits of the place
> where she had last lodged. But they were
> fine spinners in the receipt of good wages;
> and, confined all day to an atmosphere
> ranging from 75 to 80 degrees; they had
> lost all natural healthy appetite for simple
> food, and having no higher tastes, found
> their greatest enjoyment in their luxurious
> meals.

Howard's conclusion seems to be echoed by
many of the observers of the industrial city in
their attempts to understand what was happening
at a time of such phenomenal growth. The
numbers of the 'poor' had increased so dramati-
cally that they posed problems beyond the scope
of the Court Leet:

> . . . but unless we take into account all
> the poverty, destitution, and consequent in-
> ability to procure food, clothing, and
> other necessities of life, which this failing
> entails upon the working class, we shall
> form a very inadequate idea of the appall-
> ing amount of disease, misery, and crime
> which are its consequences.

> (Howard, *On the prevalence of disease*)

Mother and Child
(Tomlinson, *Bye-ways of Manchester Life*)

One of the main themes in Mrs Gaskell's story
was the life of Franky, a disabled child:

> By and by her eye fell down to gazing at
> the corresponding window to her own on
> the opposite side of the court. It was
> lighted, but the blind was drawn down.
> Upon the blind she saw, at first uncon-
> sciously, the constant weary motion of a
> little, spectral shadow; a child's hand and
> arm – no more; long, thin fingers hanging
> listlessly down, as if keeping time to the
> heavy pulses of dull pain. She could not
> help hoping that sleep would soon come
> to still that incessant, feeble motion . . .
> 'It will be Margaret Hall's lad . . . Sum-
> mat's amiss wi' his back bone, folks say;
> he's better and worse like.'

> (*Libby Marsh's Three Eras*)

The fate of such destitute children had become
a national scandal. As an inspiration to literature
they were to remain a potent source. In Manchester local authors plucked at the heart-strings
of the public, often in the pursuit of a worthy
cause.

The prolific writer, W. E. A. Axon, was
inspired to champion their cause when hearing
a speech by Mr Oakeley, Senior Inspector of

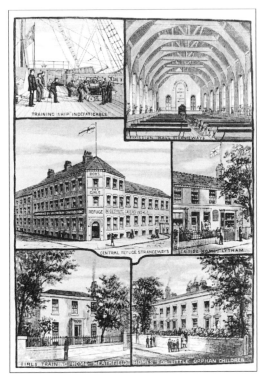

Boys' and Girls' Refuge
(Chethams, Assheton Tonge Collection)

'Oh, I'm so cold,' she murmured
(*Daddy's Bobby*)

Schools in July 1884. 'Well, where did you see a lark?' He answered, 'In the public-house at the corner of the street, in a cage.' He (Mr Oakeley) thought, 'Poor caged lark, and poor caged little lad.'

### THE ANCOATS SKYLARK

*The day was hot, the summer sun*
*Pierced through the city gloom;*
*It touched the teacher's anxious face,*
*It brightened all the room.*
*Around him children of the poor,*
*Ill fed, with clothing scant,*
*The flotsam of the social wreck,*
*The heirs of work and want.*
*The sunlight glorified their rags*
*As he essayed to tell*
*The wonders of the countryside,*
*Of clough, and burn, and fell . . .*

(*The Ancoats Skylark*)

Stories of tragic children were published in aid of local charities. *Stories of Manchester Street life*,

76

in aid of Strangways Boys and Girls Refuges and Childrens Aid Society, is typical of these.

Liz reached the corner of Oldham Street, and, crouching beside the wall of an hotel, which abuts on that street, was thus somewhat sheltered from the keen rough blasts of wind that swept along Piccadilly. Still, it was very cold; and occasionally a rougher gust than usual would sweep with a rush round the corner, sufficiently to wrench away the thin tattered skirt of her frock, which Liz had gathered around her shoulders.

It was Christmas eve; but alas, the existence of that fact brought no gladness to the poor child's heart.

'Oh, I'm so cold,' she murmured, as she drew her frock still closer to her trembling form.

(*Daddy's Bobby*)

The precise location of the tale adds authenticity

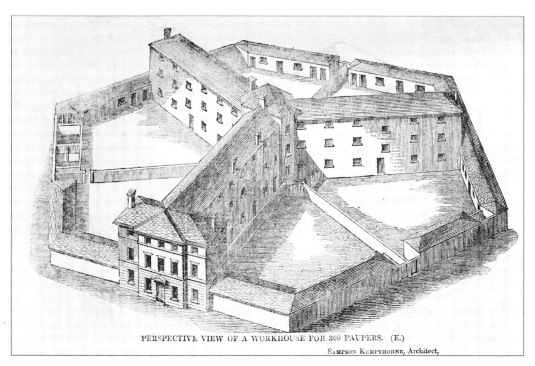

PERSPECTIVE VIEW OF A WORKHOUSE FOR 300 PAUPERS. (E.)

Sampson Kempthorne, Architect,

*(Reports of Commissioners)*

to the agony and was only mirroring the truth. Mr Herbert Taylor, a member of the Manchester Literary Club, described his own experience of the misery of street life at the turn of the century.

> On a wet autumn night I was passing through Manchester at the time the houses of entertainment were emptying. Peter Street was filled with its mighty throng of people, the shining street, lit with its thousand lamps and torches of the street, the tram-cars and the play-house, with the lights of the passing motor-cars flashing like gaudy jewels . . . As I passed along taking note of the scene, there turned out of the shadows, what in the uncertain light appeared to be a group of young boys walking with stealthy haste, unconcerned with the animation of their surroundings, there seemed a sadness, and a quiet dignity, in their movement. I looked closer, they were poor ragged boys, carrying on their shoulders a young girl, the heedless crowd made way for them, the drooping eyes of the boys suggested they were suffering a feeling of shame bravely, and wanted to pass without notice, but a passer-by said 'What is the matter?' A little boy, who was one of them, replied 'She's drunk.' They turned into the next shadow, and were swallowed in its fold.

(*Three Incidents*, Manchester Literary Club)

*Merry Christmas Gentlemen*
*'Tis thus the ancient ditty runs,*
*But nought we hear of welcome cheer,*
*For poverty's low haggard sons.*

(*The Manchester Quarterly*, 1895)

# CHAPTER 9

# 'A Very Bad Town for A Thief!'

## *Law And Order*

As Kohl reported, by the 1840s, 'Manchester is a very bad town for a thief. For if you say, in any other part of England, that you are come from Manchester, you are set down for a thief at once'.

Had this reputation always been well deserved or was it an aspect of the rapid industrialisation of the city? When it was still a country market town, the Court Leet records for Manchester show that the apprehension of law breakers and their punishment was vigorously pursued. The

first 'Beadle for the Roges' [Rogues] was appointed on 30 September 1573. Orders issued by the Court Leet covered every aspect of life in the town. Some have a modern ring, dogs were not to go about the town unmuzzled so as 'not to hurte annye of the quenes subiets ther goods & chattels'. Beggars were also a problem:

> 23 April 1584
> The Jurie doith order that wheras ther ys an order made by the Jurie in Anno

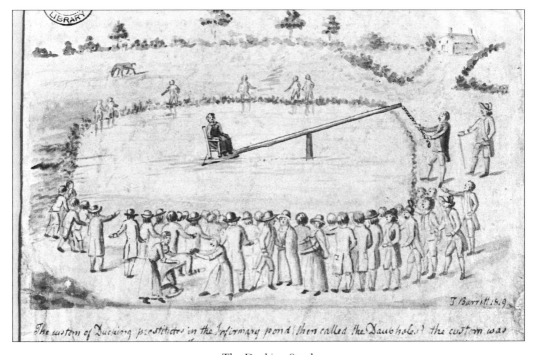

The Ducking Stool
(Chethams, Manchester Scrapbook)
'It was an open-bottomed chair of wood, placed upon a long pole (balanced on a pivot) . . . and was used
for the purpose of punishing scolds and prostitutes.'
(Axon, *Annals of Manchester*)

Radcliffe Hall, Manchester
'Otherwise the Pool House or Pool Fold Hall, which formerly stood between Cross-street chapel and
Market-street.'
(*Palatine Note-Book*)

vicessimo quarto [1582] towchinge Inmates & for the avoydinge of strange beggars & women gotten wth child & cominge vnto vs fourth of other places wher wth the towne ys verie sore pestered & burthened Inconsideraconn wherof the Jurie doith nowe order that the said order shalbe in ffull force according to effecte of the same & that the said psons appointed in said order shall see the same executed according to the same.

(*Court Leet Records*)

Single women were perceived to pose particular problems:

The Jurie doith order that wheras gret vnconvenyence ys in this towne in that se[ngle] women beinge vnmaried be at ther owne hands and do backe & brew & use other tr[ades] to the great hurte of the poor Inhabitants having wieffe & children As also in abu[sing] them selves wth yonge men & others having not anny man to controle them to the gret Dishonor of god and Evell example of others.

Women were subjected to a well known punishment – the use of the ducking stool. Manchester's stool was sited on a pond in the grounds of Radcliffe Hall. The Hall, surrounded by a moat, was half-timbered and stood in orchards and fields, on land between Cross Street and Brown Street.

The moat which surrounds the hall (as shown on the old map) or else a feeder of it, was used for the cucking-stool, it being the most convenient piece of water near the Court House . . . At Radcliffe Hall about this time [1586] was imprisoned a priest named James Bell, and it is said that his prison was in an obscure and horrid lake. The pool having become too shallow for the cuck-stool, the Horse pool at the upper end of Market-stidd-lane was used for the purpose; but in 1598 the jury of the court-leet nevertheless ordered that 'the ould accustomed place' was most convenient for the cuck-stool to stand in, and that Mr Wm Radclyffe must lay open the place again, according as heretofore it hath been used.

(Quoted in *The Palatine Notebook*)

Mr Radcliffe seems to have ignored the court's order as by 1602 they required 'a cooke-stoole to be set up in some convenient place'. It was probably at this time that the pool known as the Daubholes or the Horse Pool, in what is now Piccadilly, came into official use:

> The town also possessed stocks and a pillory. 1714 The Presbeterian Chapel, Acres-field (Cross-street) nearly destroyed by a Jacobin mob, headed by Thomas Sydall, the 'peruke [wig] maker'.
>
> 1715 The Colonel of the Manchester mob and Sydall imprisoned in the pillory.

(Quoted in *The Palatine Notebook*)

This was not a final punishment as Sydall was executed, with others, on 11 February 1716 at Liverpool. (His son was to suffer the same fate in 1746.) The pillory was in use even into the nineteenth century.

> Mr J. Galloway, sen., informs us that in 1812, about noon on Saturday, being market day, he saw the last man ever subjected to the punishment of the Pillory, standing on the table, the object of jeers and 'chaff' of the country folk who had come into the Market Place. About the same time he also saw two boatmen flogged in a cart in Deansgate, somewhere about the site of the present Free Library. These men, who had been tapping a brandy cask *en route* from London, were roped to the triangle in the cart, and received each fifty strokes from Nadin's★ cat-o'-nine-tails. Other instruments of torture existed in Manchester late on in the present century, such as the 'Scold's Bridle, or Gag' and the 'Ducking Stool'. On the authority of Mr Page, the present Superintendent of Markets, the 'Scold's Bridle' was handed over to the Corporation with the manorial rights in 1846; but, like some other property belonging to the City, it has disappeared in a mysterious

Ancient Market Cross, Stocks, and Pillory
(Axon, *Annals of Manchester*)

Scold's Bridle
(Heginbotham, *Stockport: Ancient and Modern*)

manner. The Bridle was a powerful instrument for curbing the noisy and quarrelsome tongues of the market women; and, when necessary, it was quickly and effectually applied by the officers in charge of the Markets.

(*Manchester Historical Recorder*)

★ Joseph Nadin was Deputy Constable for Manchester

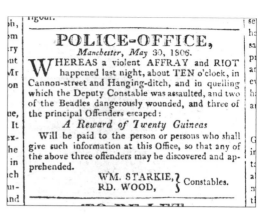

POLICE-OFFICE
(Chethams, *British Volunteer*, 7 June 1806)

Old Watchman, about 1754
(Barlow, *Historical Recorder*)

*In former days this good old town was guarded from the prigs, sir,*
*By day by constables, by night by watchmen with Welsh wigs, sir:*
*But things are altered very much, for all those who're scholars,*
*May tell the new policemen by the numbers on their collars.*
(Axon, *Lancashire Gleanings*)

Before the Police force was established, Manchester had two separate bodies of men to guard the town which was divided into districts. The system had been established under the manorial Court Leet: during the day constables were responsible for law and order, at night watchmen took over. Their function was 'to secure the peace of the town, prosecute offenders, put down unlawful games, make faithful presentment of 'all bloodsheds, outcries, affrays, and rescues'.

These were honorary positions, which could also be dangerous:

Michaelmas, 26 Elizabeth 1584
there was a brawl made, and blood drawn upon the watchmen. The constables had the parties before them that made the brawl, and have made no presentment; therefore we present them [the constables] to have been negligent in doing their duty.

(*Court Leet Records*)

Policing the city was under the control of a special commission which had to go to great lengths to maintain daily surveillance:

The number of watchmen allowed by the Commissioners of the Police for the Town of Manchester is seventy-four, & nine supernumeraries, in case any of the others are sick or absent . . . and make their reports, as cases may be, to the Police-officers, who attend for the above purposes; and likewise the said officers attend at the office in King-street, from half-past eight in the morning, till one, and from two until seven in the evening, to execute the orders, and transact the business of the police, every day (Sunday excepted). There is a Lock-up House at the corner of St George's-road & Swan-street: a patrol of five watchmen is established in St George's-road and Oldham-road.

(*The Manchester Directory*)

Charge Office, Goulden Street, 1887
(Tomlinson, *Bye-ways of Manchester*)

Kohl arranged a private visit to a police-office:

> It was half underground, and was reached by a descending flight of steps. It consisted of rooms, in which the police commissioners sat as judges, although it was twelve o'clock at night, and behind were several *lock-ups*, as the temporary prisons of the police-offices are called. At Manchester, there are in winter 300, and in summer 250 policemen in constant attendance . . . Behind the bars of the lock-up sat several drunken fellows, who were swearing and quarrelling in a frightful manner, so that the noise rang through the subterranean vaults. In the same cell as these wretches, were shut up a couple of little boys.

> (*Ireland, Scotland and England*)

According to Aston, the earliest prison had been 'the chapel on the Old Bridge, mentioned by

Leland'. This was known locally as 'The Dungeon' and used until 1778:

> It was situated on the north side of the bridge, upon the middle pier, and consisted of two apartments, one over the other. In this prison accused felons, deserters, and other military culprits were confined. They who were so unfortunate as to be lodged in the lower dungeon, were often in the most perilous situation, from the rise of the river by floods.

> (Aston, *A Picture of Manchester*)

A second prison had been in use since Elizabethan times, the House of Correction, on Hunt's Bank:

> It was first used for the purpose of confining popish recusants; but afterwards became the regular prison for the Hundreds of Salford.

This building was replaced by the New Bailey in 1790. Situated in Stanley Street, Salford, it served both towns, for all offences except capital, for a population Aston estimates as 300,000. In 1816, when *A Picture of Manchester* was going to press, a footnote explains that the size of the prison was being doubled because 'Such is the increase of depravity with the increase of population and prosperity of the Hundred of Salford.' Aston's conjecture seems to be borne out by a table of prisoners tried in Salford in Love's *Manchester as it is* (1839).

| 1794 | 150 | 1815 | 497 | 1830 | 842 |
|------|-----|------|-----|------|-----|
| 1800 | 441 | 1820 | 906 | 1834 | 1112 |
| 1805 | 252 | 1825 | 993 | 1836 | 1031 |
| 1810 | 241 | 1827 | 983 | 1837 | 1313 |

Once committed, prisoners were made to work and by 1816 there were fifty-three workshops within the prison:

. . . if he is committed for twelve months certain, he is taught to weave; and on his discharge, if he had previously no regular employment, he will be able to earn his livelihood in an honest manner, as a dimity weaver. This provision is true humanity! and cold and unfeeling must be the heart which does not pay it the tribute of applause.

(Love, *Manchester as it is*)

On discharge some of the prisoners' earnings were given to them to 'enable them to subsist until they can find work'.

A contemporary description of the New Bailey is given in a book published in 1819 by Joseph John Gurney, the Quaker prison reformer. He and his sister, Elizabeth Fry, visited Manchester on the 26 September 1818. The prisoners were in good health, the prison well ventilated and frequently whitewashed. The prison was properly supplied with 'Bibles and Testaments'.

House of Correction, Hunt's Bank, about 1776
(Procter, *Memorials of Manchester Streets*)
'The prisoners, by the help of bags let down from the grated windows, were almost constantly employed in soliciting the charity of passengers . . . The profits of their petitionary bags, were but too often exchanged for spirituous liquors . . .'
(Aston, *A Picture of Manchester*)

New Bayley, Salford, and River Irwell
(Gregson, *Portfolio of Fragments*)
'The first stone was laid by the late T. B. Bayley, Esq. which gave rise to the mistaken notion in the minds
of many persons, as to the etymology of the name of the prison, and it has generally been called the New
"Bayley" instead of the New "Bailey" prison which is the proper designation.'
(Aston, *Picture of Manchester*)

The prisoners are supplied with firing, and the felons and convicts have a jail dress. Their food is as follows: one pound and a half of bread daily; for breakfast a quart of oatmeal gruel, the same for supper; for dinner (on three days) half a pound of beef and one pound of potatoes; on three other days, a quart of pease soup, and on the remaining day, a quart of broth or stew. This allowance of food appears more than sufficiently plentiful for those prisoners who are unemployed. The governor however considers that it prevents disease; an opinion which is supported by the fact, that there has been only one instance in the prison of infectious fever during the last twenty-four years and this instance was occasioned by the admission of an infected prisoner. This circumstance is the more remarkable, as the prison has on occasions been crowded to excess. Before the new buildings were erected *752*

*persons were at one period confined in 150 cells, those cells being severally intended only for one inmate!*

(*Notes on a visit*)

Even though the prison seems to have been forward looking Gurney did not feel Manchester was a reforming prison:

At present, it is too clearly proved by the number of recommitment, *which form more than a fourth part of the commitments*, that the New Bailey cannot be numbered amongst the houses of reform. The corruption of morals, which prevails in Manchester and its neighbourhood, is indeed terrible. The district for which the New Bailey serves as a prison is said to contain 250,000 inhabitants; and I am informed by the governor, that no less than 2,500 offenders of various descriptions, that is, *one hundredth part of the*

Above: Two Houses Wanted
(Chethams, *Courier*, 9 July 1825)
Right: House of Correction, Salford
(Chethams, *Courier*, 7 May, 1827)

*whole population*, pass through this jail in
the course of the year . . .

(Gurney, *Notes on a visit*)

Kohl thought that prison visiting was a useful way
for travellers to become acquainted with the
'character and condition of the people, this is
peculiarly the case in England, where the super-
intendents of the prisons are always so liberal in
affording him opportunities and assistance'. He
visited the New Bailey, extended again in 1826,
claiming it was one of 'the most extensive, important, and interesting prisons in the country'.

When I was in the New Bailey, almost all
the solitary cells were filled with boys who
had committed fresh offenses since entering
the prison, and were consequently, con-
demned to solitary confinement; . . . The
guilt of these children rests of course ulti-
mately upon the neglect and immorality of
their parents. One of the boys formerly an
industrious and well-behaved lad had
become a thief out of sheer desperation
and want, because his drunken father de-
prived him by force of his weeks wages
every Saturday night, and then left him to
suffer the most bitter privations for want of
it. An interesting investigation, lately made
at Manchester places the responsibility of
the parents in the clearest light. Out of
100 poor children who had committed
crimes, there were:

Children of dishonest and profligate parents, 60
profligate but not dishonest parents, 30
respectable and industrious parents, 10
———
100

(*Ireland, Scotland and England*)

Kohl does observe that the New Bailey was
'clean, spacious and airy' and that the diet was
superior to that of the poor – a reason he postu-
lates for the high numbers of returning criminals:

The following is the weekly provision of
a full-grown prisoner, in the Manchester
New Bailey.

| | s. | d. |
|---|---|---|
| Seven loaves of twenty ounces each, costing | 1 | 1 |
| Thirty-one ounces of flour | 0 | 4 |
| Five pounds of potatoes | 0 | 1 |
| One pint of pease | 0 | 1 |
| Three ounces and a half of salt | 0 | 0 |
| One pound of beef | 0 | 4 |
| One quart of beer | 0 | 0 |
| | 1 | 11 |

Gurney, too, had concluded that 'the Manchester
thief is well fed on gruel and broth, and bread
and cheese'.

Prisoners did not usually stay long in the New
Bailey, being sent to other local jails, transported
or released. Kohl encountered a 'contractor for
removing the convicts' on his visit. The govern-
ment was not responsible for this trade but 'private speculators':

. . . the governor of that prison gives
public notice that he has so many
prisoners to transport to such a place, and
that the conveyance will be entrusted to
whoever will undertake it at the lowest
price. The contractor of course must give
security, that he will deliver the right number at the right time and the right place,
undamaged and in good condition; but
otherwise he may do what he pleases with

Newgate, Prison Discipline
(Adshead, *Prison and Prisoners*)

them . . . Formerly the contractors used large vans for this purpose, but of late they generally hire the horse-boxes of the railway trains, which are fitted up with benches for the purpose. Two hundred and fifty criminals are annually transported in this way from the New Bailey in Manchester.

(*Ireland, Scotland and England*)

Kohl had been concerned, like Gurney, by the number of children in Manchester's prisons:

More than half the entire population of Manchester is under twenty-three years of age.

In the year 1841 were convicted and sentenced to transportation in Manchester alone, 177 children under seventeen years of age. Eighty-seven boys and fifteen girls were sentenced to seven years transportation, fifty-five boys and five girls to ten years, and twenty-six boys to fifteen years.

Youthful criminals were thought to be of 'confirmed bad habits' and beyond redemption. There was schooling provided in the prison and

Apprehending a criminal
(Chethams *Momus*)

86

Kohl talked to 'the good old school-master' who kept a journal of his 'depraved young scholars'. The old man showed Christian charity as he helped parents keep in touch with their children when they had been sentenced to transportation. A mother's letter gives an insight into the harsh reality of family separation:

> How it grieves me, my dear son, that you had such a stormy passage to Australia. I thought something must have happened to you, as you did not write to me. My little shop does not go a bit better; on the contrary, it is worse this year than the last, and every thing grows worse here every year. I feel very comfortable with James, for we have family prayers together twice a day, every morning and every evening. God be with you my dear son. Your affectionate mother, &c.

# CHAPTER 10

# 'The Wakes! The Wakes! The Jocund Wakes!'

## Pastimes

The Bag-piper
From a sculptured panel at Hulme Hall.
(*The Palatine Notebook*)

*The Lancashire Bagpiper*
*He.*
*Blowzabella, my bouncing doxy,*
*Come, let's trudge it to Kirkham Fair;*
*There's stout liquor enough to fox me,*
*And young cullies to buy thy ware.*

(Harland, *Ballads & Songs of Lancashire*)

James I issued a declaration giving license to Lancashire people 'that *Women* should have leave to carry *Rushes* to the Church, for the Decorating it according to their custom'. (Fiellis, *Church History* quoted in *Rush Bearing*)

The riot and debaucheries which eventually took place at these nocturnal meetings became so offensive to the pious that the church authorities attempted to suppress them:

> In Manchester, during these holidays, the pageants of Robin Hood, Maid Marian, and Friar Tuck, were exhibited in the church, and were generally got up by the priests. The expense of these exhibitions were defrayed by the church-wardens, who made collections from house to house for that object.
> In 1579, an assembly of ecclesiastical commissioners held at Manchester, issued a mandate against pipers and minstrels making and frequenting bear-baiting and bull-baiting on the Sabbath days, or upon any other days, and also against superstitious ringing of bells, *wakes*, and other common feasts, drunkenness, gaming, and other vicious and unprofitable pursuits.

(Burton, *Rush Bearing*)

Though working hours were long, and workers rarely well paid, Mancunians always found time to enjoy themselves. The 'Wakes' were originally festivals commemorating the Saint's Day of the local church's foundation when rushes were taken to the church to cover the floor. This developed into a religious procession on the occasion of the church's dedication. In 1617

The population protested and in 1633, Charles I warranted that 'the Feasts of the Dedication of the Churches, commonly called Wakes shall be observed', and regular fairs established to be held on the saint's day. Over time the custom of rush-bearing became formalised into the building of rush cats to elaborate designs.

A Lancashire Rushcart
(Burton, *Rush-Bearing*)
The accompanying view of such a scene is taken from a fine picture, painted by Alexander Wilson, in 1821 (formerly in the possession of Mr Roger Wilson, of Woodford, Cheshire), representing a rush-cart in Long Millgate, Manchester. The canvas is studied with characteristic figures, inclusive of the artist himself (his bandaged foot required temporary crutches).
(Burton, *Rush-Bearing*. Also Procter, *Memorials of Manchester Streets*)

*The Wakes! the Wakes! the jocund Wakes!*
*My wondering memory now forsakes*
*This present busy scene of things*
*Erratic, upon farey's wings,*
*For olden times with garlands crown'd*
*And rushcarts green as many a mound.*

(Quoted in Brierley, *Daisy Nook Sketches*)

Manchester had no rush-cart of its own, but every year a number of carts visited from the neighbouring towns, some coming from as far as Oldham and Rochdale:

On the 31st August, 1882, a rush-cart from Oldham came to Manchester, and paraded the principal streets about five o'-clock in the afternoon. It was made in an ordinary two-wheeled cart. The angles were feathered, and formed of rods about an inch thick, the tops projecting about a foot and painted blue. On the top of the cart, almost hidden by a great bough of oak, was a little man with a very dirty face, and wearing a red jacket. The sides of the cart were plain, on the back, 'V.R.', formed of yellow flowers stuck in the rushes.

(Burton, *Rush-Bearing*)

Ben Brierly vividly describes his experiences on wakes day:

I had a blue sash, which had done good service in odd-fellowship, fastened over my left shoulder, and tied by a bow under my left arm. A rosette about the dimensions of a target hung upon my

Bear-Baiting at Hyde's Cross
(Burton, *Rush-Bearing*)
'the wakes without a bait of some kind was considered a farce. Bull-baiting was the one most in vogue. A well-trained dog ran under the bull's legs, and pinned it by the lips . . . In bear-baiting, the above tactics would not do, and a good dog at a bull would make but a poor show with a bear, who had to be pinned before he could use his claws.'
(Burton, *Rush-Bearing*)

A Rush Cart. From a letter: Jessee Lee to Hones' Year Book, 4 May 1825 (Burton, *Rush-Bearing*)

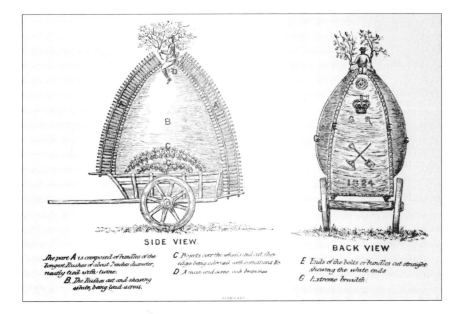

90

FIG. 116. Toxophilite uniform, 1792
(*Print by Rowlandson in 'Men,*

An archer of 1792
(Print by Rowlandson in 'Men, Maidens,
and Manners'.
'The Woodmen of Arden, Broughton Archers, and
Lancashire Bowmen united in holding a meeting at
Cannock Chase in 1791, apparently a second meet-
ing took place in 1792.'
(Badminton Library, *Archery*)

breast, and every part of my body where
a ribbon could be fastened had an ample
streamer floating from it. Add to my gear
a large peacock's feather, which was stuck
in front of my hat, and waved over a
crown made of wire and neck-beads, and
little more would be required to give you
a perfect idea of the costume in which I
appeared on that auspicious Wakes Day.

Our 'cart', which was a box about four
feet long, mounted on wheels, and built
up with rushes until it had the appearance

of having 'water in the head', was now declared to be ready. The sheet was fastened
to the front; sunflowers and hollyhocks
were stuck in the rear, and a youngster
about the size of a milking-stool was
mounted straddle-leg on the top; and
what from the ribbons he wore, and the
foliage of the oak boughs which were
stuck on each apex of the cart. The little
fellow looked like a very Jack-in-the-
green on a small scale.

'Howd up yo'r wagues!' was the signal
given to start. Away we go over knolls
and gutters; children shouting, old women
screaming, and the band going it like mad.

(Brierley, *Daisy Nook Sketches*)

Another activity associated with holy-days was
archery. Bowmen had been required to practise
so they would be ready if there was a national
call to arms. As Agincourt became a memory
the practice fell into neglect:

Also yt is Ordered that the inhabiters
within the town of mamchestre shall make
or cause to be made too peyre of Butts
that ys to saye the inhabytants vpon the
Southe side of the churche to make one
peyre of butts in the marketstede Lane,
And thenhabitants [*sic*] of the north side of
the churche one other peyre of butts vpo
Colyhurste afore the feast of Sainet John
Bapt [June 24] nexte comynge, Sub pena
to either of theme that make defaute vjs.
viijd. (6s. 8d.)

(*Court Leet Records*, 1561)

The constables enforced the Act of 1541 and as
holy days were often free from work this became
the day spent at the butts. Practice began early
in life, from seven to seventeen, males were
required to have a bow and two arrows, from
eighteen to seventy, a bow and four arrows –
or the Court Leet could levy fines. By the
nineteenth century archery had become a sport
and clubs established nationwide. The most famous Manchester club, the Broughton Archers
founded in the eighteenth century, was an exclusive society. Building on the local tradition of
archery, meetings were held at the Turf Tavern

Chetham Library 1797
(*Memorials of Manchester Streets*)

Kersal Moor which had a dining room used by club members as well as the archery ground.

There are echoes of the early training for boys in the recollections of George Morwood a pupil at Manchester Free Grammar School:

> It was then the usual custom of the school [Manchester Free Grammar School], on Shrove [or Pancake] Tuesday, for the boys to shoot with bows and arrows for prizes. Certainly the first three days of Shrovetide, perhaps all the working days of the week, were kept as a holiday; and on the Tuesday, perhaps at ten o'clock in the morning, the lads, then about two hundred in number, assembled in a field on the banks of the Irk; crossing the river over the foot-bridge by a steep declivity from Long Millgate, the field being a little higher up the river than the bridge . . . The four lower classes, in the early school days of our informant, shot with bows and arrows at living cocks, which were

so placed in holes in the ground covered with turf, that the head and part of the neck of the bird only were visible above the turf. The boys shot in succession, at the distance of perhaps thirty yards, at the exposed head and neck of the poor bird, and he who first 'drew blood' had the cock for his prize. This practice of shooting at a living cock was however discontinued, Mr M. is pretty sure, in the second year of his attendance there, which would be in the year 1772–3.

(Harland, *Collectanea*)

Morwood seems to have had an interesting time at school as hunting was another of his activities. This seemingly unlikely Manchester sport shows how immediate the town was to the countryside in the eighteenth century:

> I remember seeing an old map, with a picture in one corner of it, as maps have even now-a-days. In this picture were represented certain persons in the dress of

The Manchester or Lancashire hound
(Whitaker, *History*)

A TEA PARTY.

A Tea Party
'Of course they paid visits – how could women live
without a little gossip?'
(Ashton, *Social Life in the Reign of Queen Anne*)

*And for the third, wherein fhe doth all fhires*
*exceed,*
*Be thofe great race of hounds, the deepeft-mouthed*
*of all*
*The others of this kind which we our Hunters call;*
*Which from their bellowing throats upon a fent fo*
*roare,*
*That you would furely thinke that the firme earth*
*they tore*
*With their wide yawning chaps, or rent the clouds*
*in funder,*
*As though by their lowd crie they meante to*
*mocke the thunder.*
(Drayton, quoted in Whitaker, *History*)

Queen Anne's time, on foot, with leaping
poles in their hands, hunting the hare in
some fields on the banks of the river Irk,
opposite the Grammar School Mills. I can
remember hunting myself with the old
Manchester Harriers. They were very large
dogs, much larger than the present fox-
hound, remarkable for the melody of their
voice, very slow, but very sure in their
operation. When one of these dogs got
upon the scent, he would squat upon his
haunches, and with the greatest gravity,
give tongue most melodiously; having fin-
ished his tune, he commenced hunting
with equal deliberation, but was always
successful. The last of these hounds which

I saw was in a pack of very swift harriers,
with which he cut a very queer figure.
This pack belonged to the late Mr Aldous
Parker, of Retford, Notts, who had pro-
cured the dog with great difficulty, and
prized him highly for the melody of his
voice.

More genteel pastimes had been established
within the town – though not all the inhabitants
were won over to them:

From an early period in the eighteenth
century, the amusements of the inhabitants of Manchester consisted of cards,
balls, theatrical performances, and con-
certs. About 1720 a wealthy lady named
Madam Drake, who kept one of three
or four private carriages that existed in
the town, refused to conform to the
new beverages of tea and coffee; so that,
whenever she made an afternoon's visit,
her friends presented her with that to
which she had been accustomed,– a tan-
kard of ale and a pipe of tobacco! The
usual entertainment at gentlemen's houses
at that period included wet and dry
sweetmeats, different sorts of cake and
gingerbread, apples, or other fruits of the
season, and a variety of home-made
wines . . .

(Chambers, *The Book of Days*)

By the nineteenth century Manchester's entertainments were very diverse: theatres, clubs, libraries, an Assembly room on Mosley Street, and an annual social calender of balls and music, together with sporting activities, inns and taverns. For most of the population Sunday was still the only day of the week free from work. Hugh Miller determined to examine how the population enjoyed the day:

> I lodged within a stone-cast of the terminus of the Great Manchester and Birmingham Railway . . . I sauntered down to the gate by which a return train was discharging its hundreds of passengers, fresh from the Sabbath amusements of the country, that I might see how they looked. There did not seem much of enjoyment about the wearied and somewhat draggled groups . . . There was not much actual drunkenness among the crowd,– thanks to the preference which the Englishman gives to his ale over ardent spirits,– not a tithe of what I would have witnessed, on a similar occasion in my own country [Scotland] . . . With the humble Englishman, trained up to no regular habit of church-going, Sabbath is pudding-day, and clean-shirt-day, and a day for lolling on the grass opposite the sun, and, if there be a river or canal hard by, for trying how the gudgeon bite, or if in the neighbourhood of a railway, for taking a short trip to some country inn, famous for its cakes and ale . . .
>
> (*First Impressions*)

Had Miller arrived at Whitsuntide he might have recorded a different Manchester:

> Whitsuntide in Manchester, is the Annual Jubilee. Beside the fair and the races, plays, concerts, assemblies, and that cruel unmanly sport, cock-fighting, make out the amusements of the week. Business is nearly at a stand; and Pleasure reigns with almost Parisian despotism.
>
> (Aston, *Picture of Manchester*)

'Whit-week' as it was known had grown to be the great yearly holiday of the hundred of Sal-

Manchester Races
(Chethams, *Courier*, 5 June 1819)

ford. This seems to have arisen from the yearly races at Manchester being held from the Wednesday to the Saturday inclusive in that week. The races, held on Kersal Moor, had started about 1730. They had aroused opposition, especially from Dr Byrom – and in 1745 they were discontinued. Fifteen years later they were re-established and continued to grow in popularity:

> Horse Races, are annually held at Whitsuntide; . . . The race-ground is upon Kersal Moor, about three miles north-west from the town . . . When the astonishing concourse of people who attend this diversion upon Kersal Moor is considered, and which almost sets any calculation of their numbers at defiance, it may fairly be said, that the pleasures of no races in England, are embittered by the recollection of

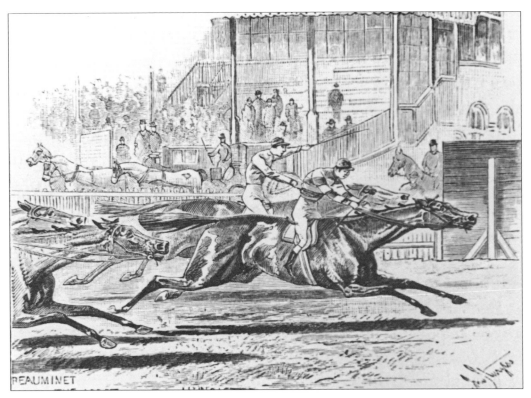

'Without the use of either whip or spur.'
(Badminton Library, *Racing*)

fewer accidents happening to the specta-
tors than those of Manchester.

(Aston, *Picture of Manchester*)

By mid-century the week was a well-established
holiday with its own traditions and events:

It is customary for the cotton-mills &c., to
close for Whitsun-tide week to give the
hands a holiday; the men going to the
races &c., and the women visiting Manchester on Whit-Saturday, thronging the markets, the Royal Exchange, the Infirmary
Esplanade, and other public places; and gazing in at the 'shop windows', whence this
day is usually called 'Gaping Saturday'.

(Harland, *Lancashire Folklore*)

The week was always seen as an opportunity to
take outings away from Manchester, first to the
fields around the town then as transport improved to more distant vistas.

The extension of the railway system has
led to 'cheap trips' and 'school excursion
trains' during Whitsuntide; which are occasionally taken to Wales, the Lakes and
other great distances. Canal boats take
large numbers of Sunday scholars to Dunham Park, Worsley, &c. Short excursions
are taken in carts, temporarily fitted with
seats.

(Harland, *Lancashire Folklore*)

Mrs Gaskell describes such a trip in *Libby Marsh's
Three Eras* as the friends embark on the canal to
visit Dunham, near Altrincham:

Away went the boat to make room for
the others; for every conveyance both by
land and by water is in requisition in
Whitsun-week to give the hard-worked
crowds an opportunity of tasting the
charms of the country. Even every standing place in the canal packets was occupied; and as they glided along, the banks

Oldfield, Dunham
(Grindon, *Country Rambles*)

were lined with people, who seemed to
find it object enough to watch the boats
go by packed close and full with happy
beings brimming with anticipation of a
day's pleasure. The country through
which they passed is as uninteresting as
can well be imagined, but still it is
'country' and the screams of delight
from the children, and the low laughs of
pleasure from the parents, at every blos-
soming tree which trailed its wreaths,
against some cottage-wall, or at the tufts
of late primroses which lingered in the
cool depths of grass along the canal
banks the thorough relish of everything,
as if dreading to let the least circumstances on this happy day pass without
its due appreciation made the time seem
all too short, although it only took two
hours to arrive at a place only eight
miles distant from Manchester . . . 'Oh,
Libbie how beautiful! Oh, mother,
mother! Is the whole world out of Manchester as beautiful as this! . . .'

Richard Buxton, one of Manchester's working-
class botanists writing in 1849, was convinced
of the pleasure to be gained by his fellow workers

A Country Stroll
(Waugh, *Poems and Songs*)

in 'exploring the wonders of nature, after a week
of labour':

During the last forty years, the face of the
country around Manchester is, no doubt,

greatly changed. However, there yet remain the well-wooded and pleasant valleys of the Etherow and Goyt, and out of the latter a charming little dell at Fog Brook; the picturesque valley of the Tame, by Reddish, through Haughton, and Staly, to the romantic rocks of Greenfield, in Saddleworth. Then there are the quiet dingles of Boggart-hole, Prestwich, and Mere Cloughs; the meadows of Agecroft and Clifton; the vales of the Irwell, Irk, and Medlock; the deep valleys of Healey, Ashworth, Bamford, Bradshaw, Sharples, and many others; the rural villages of Chorlton-cum-Hardy, Didsbury, Northen, and Sale; and lastly, the delightful valley of the Bollin, and Cotterill Clough.

(Buxton, *Botanical Guide*)

There were, however, objections to the activities of 'Whit-week' that are reminders of the sixteenth-century protests at the wakes, and the eighteenth-century diatribes of Dr Byrom against the races.

After the rise of Sunday-schools, their conductors, desiring to keep youth of both sexes from the demoralising recreations of the racecourse, took them to the fields in the neighbourhood and held anniversary celebrations, tea-parties &c., in the schools.

(Harland, *Lancashire Folklore*)

When His Honour Judge Parry moved to Manchester in 1886 he found he had chosen an inauspicious week:

I moved down to Manchester in Whit-week – or tried to. For Manchester has an excellent and sacred custom in Whit-week. Nobody does any work . . . For the shops close, the workman goes to Blackpool or the Isle of Man, and the employer to Paris or the West Highlands, or St Andrews, or North Berwick as the mood suggests, and Lancashire and Yorkshire play cricket at Old Trafford and the races are run, and the children dressed in white, carrying their banners, move in procession through streets thronged with admiring parents. And that all may be at

peace and good will the Protestant children 'walk' – that is the Manchester word – on one day and the Roman Catholics on another, for fear the good Christian parents of either denomination should batter each other's skulls whilst their little children sing 'Lead Kindly Light'.

(Parry, *What the Judge Saw*)

All the elements were there: days out, religious processions, and sport.

One sport which did not yet officially feature in the celebrations, was becoming increasingly important to the life of the city – football.

Parry might comment on the battling parents but disorder had long been associated with holidays in Manchester. The football hooligan was abroad in the streets of the town as early as 1608:

That whereas there hath been heretofore great disorder in our towne of Manchester, and the inhabitants thereof greatly wronged and charged with makinge and amendinge of their glasse windows broken yearelye and spoyled by a company of lewd and disordered psons vsing that unlawfull exercise of playinge with the ffote-ball in ye streets of ye sd toune breakinge many men's windowes and glasse at their plesures and other great enormyties. Therefore, wee of this jurye doe order that no manner of psons hereafter shall play or use the footeball in any street within the said toune of Manchester, subpoend to evye one that shall so use the same for evye time xiid. [12d.].

(Manchester Lete Roll, 12 October 1608. Quoted in *Athletics and Football*, Badminton Library)

As Manchester grew so did a large youthful population, many societies were founded to encourage more 'worthwhile' activities for them; Heyrod Street Lads Club, Ancoats was one of them. Charles Russell, the Honourary Secretary in his account of 'Manchester Lads at Work and Play' has a view of football not entirely enthusiastic:

To many Manchester lads, outdoor games have only one meaning, and that is

Above: The Association Game
Below: 'The field at each kick changes like a kaleidoscope.'
'The one generally admitted drawback to the game is the frequency of the disputes which arise . . .'
(Both from Badminton Library, *Athletics and Football*)

The Day at Alderley
(Smith, *Pilgrim Street*)

There is also a lamentable lack of any fine sense of sportsmanship to be noticed . . . Cricket, for Manchester lads at any rate, has nothing like the same attraction as football.

(Russell, *Manchester Boys*)

B. A. Redfern, a contributor to the Manchester Literary Club, was more sympathetic.:

I had not been on 'Th' Owd Buryin' Ground' . . . until a certain day of mid-summer at the beginning of this century, when I was returning by rail from a tramp on the moorlands about 'Bill's o' Jackes' and was nearing Victoria Station, I saw from the carriage window what induced me to visit the old ground on my way home.

Entering it by a flight of wide steps I came out upon a great flagged space, lit up with the glow of a rich sunset, and found it swarming with children of all ages and sizes . . .

At the lower, and more level, end of the flagged space, where a long row of railway arches and several great gasometers bounded the view, scores of yelling and perspiring lads, chiefly with uncovered heads and feet attired in mere apologies for garments, were playing games,– recognis-able as 'staggit,' 'relieve oh!' 'slap-ear,' 'leap frog,' and the like,– as if each player's life depended on his individual efforts. Elder boys and youths, of a type which in later life supply our 'hooligans,' were playing football, here with a real ball, and there with one made of impacted paper (or of an old hat), bound with string. It was an exhilarating sight, and a much more interesting one to me than would have been that of a match between the so called 'City' and the 'United,' and I stayed to enjoy it for a few exciting minutes.

football, as played under the Association Code. Football is as popular in summer as in winter, and were it not for the fact that the rules governing the game prohibit the playing of matches during the summer months it would be played from ones year's end to another. As it is, in the arti-san quarters of the city, boys attempt to play the game in the heat of the summer with small balls or tightly rolled up bundles of paper; . . . The game is usually played with considerable vigour, and where the boys are not under proper con-trol the language and conduct of the players leave a very great deal to be desired. Tempers are easily aroused, and a boy often neglects an opportunity of really playing the game well in order that he may, as he terms it, 'get his own back' for an injury inflicted upon himself, earlier in the game, perhaps quite accidentally.

This prospect of children at play amid 'disenchanting slums', was for Redfern a 'City Idyll'.

# CHAPTER 11

# 'Ring Out The Old'

## *A Lost Manchester*

The custom of ringing regular peals now peculiar to the inhabitants of England, commenced in the time of the Saxons, and was common before the Conquest.

(Whitaker, *History*)

Whitaker attributed the custom of bell ringing, as he did so many other customs, to the Romans:

Bells were used by the Romans to signify the times of bathing, and naturally applied by the Christians of Italy, therefore to denote the hours of devotion and summon the people to the church. They were so applied before the conclusion of the seventh century in the monastick societies of Northumbria . . .

Whatever the origins, by the seventeenth century bell-ringing had become well established and a source of dispute in Manchester:

1679 Wee . . . Churchwardens of ye Towneand Parish of Manchester, etc. Haveinge on this our year beene att greate and yett Nessessary Charges and Expence in casting all the bells new belonging to the parrish Church of Manchester, and fynding that by Reason of the Neglect, and Thorough the Carelessness of the Clerks belonging to the sd Church, who for their owne Gaine and Advantage have frequently suffered yonge Youthes, and persons wholly inexperianced in Ringing soe that heretofore the bells have been much Dammaged, burst, and spoyld, whereby the parish have been put to great Charges in Repairing of them.

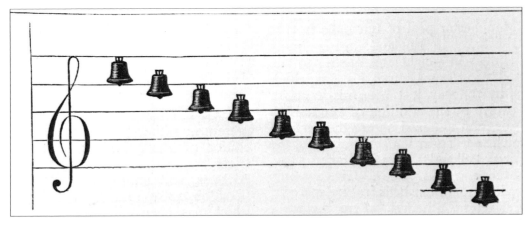

The Ringing Peal at the Town Hall, Manchester
'The best time to judge the quality of these fine bells is on that particular Sunday in November, when the newly-elected Mayor attends divine service at the Cathedral. It is then possible to hear simultaneously the Cathedral bells in the key of D sharp; the bells of Sacred Trinity, Salford, in F; the bells of St John's Deansgate, in A; and dominating over all, the grand tones of the Town Hall bells in C.'
*(Palatine Notebook)*

Mrs Raffald
(Chethams, Manchester Scrapbook)
'At first, we believe, Mrs Raffald kept a
confectioner's shop at the corner of Exchange Alley.'
(Harland, *Collectanea*)

We . . . have made Choyce of a certaine number of Ringers, who are conceived to be men expert in Ringing, and they are to be allowed for evry peall they ring 4d., being not one under one quarter of an hour.

(*Churchwardens' Accounts*)

Bells were not confined to use in churches, nor to summoning to prayer, but in the eighteenth century were put to more mundane purposes:

Where Exchange street is now [1850] was Newton's, the bookseller, where the gentlemen of the town used to go in order to know what the bells were ringing for. The fashion was at that time, to send a guinea or two to the ringers, when a man had brought his wife to the town.

(Harland, *Collectanea*)

Newton's and the coffee shop next door were at the corner of Exchange Alley at the very centre of Manchester's busy shopping area with the Market Place, the Apple Market and Smithy Door close by. And at the very centre of the centre (possibly at the coffeee house) was Mrs Raffald:

. . . the mere mention of her name suggests to the epicurean vision glorious dreams of the meats and dishes with which she was wont to minister to the toothsome tastes of our good Manchester citizens and their fair wives and sisters . . .

(*Palatine Notebooks*)

In 1769 Harrop's *Mercury* announced:

An entire new Work, Wrote for the Use and Ease of Ladies, House-Keepers, Cooks, etc. entitled The EXPERIENCED ENGLISH House-Keeper. By Elizabeth Raffald. Wrote purely from Practice, and Dedicated to the Hon. *Elizabeth Warburton*, Whom the Author lately served as House-keeper. Consisting of near 800 Original Receipts, most of which never appeared in Print.

(Quoted in *Palatine Notebook*)

*The Experienced English House-Keeper* was such a success that it attracted a London publisher, R. Baldwin, who paid £1400 in cash for the copyright. The formidable Mrs Raffald was not however to be intimidated by the man from the south:

when Mr Baldwin had handed the notes to Mrs Raffald, he observed to her that there were several term in the book which were in general use in the north, but which he was sure would not be understood in the south; and he therefore respectfully asked her permission to be allowed to alter them. Mrs Raffald, who is described as a fine, dignified, lady-like woman . . . drew herself up, as she was wont when her dignity was ruffled, and said with a marked emphasis: 'What I have written I proposed to write at the time; it was written deliberately, and I cannot admit to any alteration.'

(Harland, *Collectanea*)

Besides the compendious advice on housekeeping, Mrs Raffald produced one of the first

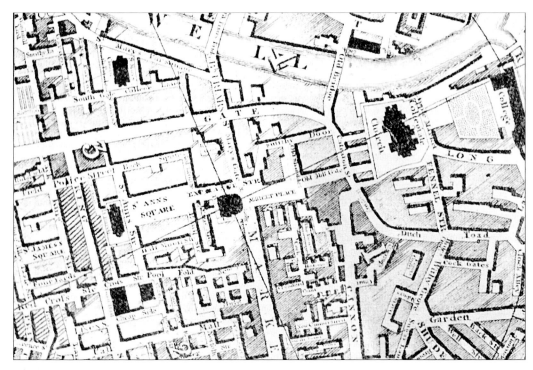

Map of central Manchester showing Smithy Door and environs, about 1800
(Slugg, *Reminiscences*)

directories of Manchester (and seventeen children!) while also running a very successful inn, first the Bull's Head in the Market place, then the King's Head, Salford. Both acted as the regimental messes for officers stationed in the town. The Bull's Head was also the meeting place for the boys from the Free Grammar School but only once a year – officially. The inn was the destination for the Easter parade after the scholar's archery practice at the 'dunghill cock'.

> The procession returned along Hunt's Bank, the Apple Market, Fennel Street, Hanging Ditch and Old Millgate to the Bull's Head . . . where the junior boys were treated with *frumerty* – wheat stewed and then boiled in milk with raisin, currants, and spices, till it forms a thick porridge-like mess, exceedingly palatable to the young folk. The masters and assistants, and the senior scholars, partook of roast beef, plum puddings, etc.
>
> (Harland, *Lancashire Folk Lore*)

The abolition of this custom early in the nineteenth century 'was by no means relished by the Grammar School boys'. With the ringing of bells, the throng of soldiers, traders, schoolboys and shoppers, the whole area must have been a bustle of restless energy, its focus the Smithy Door:

> The Old Millgate, some years since was only accounted a road on sufferance; but it was so crowded with carriages (and carts) on a market-day, that it was dangerous to pass them; and the Smithy Door, which was the proper road to Salford Bridge, being also wedged up with throngs meeting, like two opposite currents, there appeared to be yet a necessity of removing the market-people, either wholly or in part, to some other situation.
>
> (Harland, *Collectanea*)

The houses and shops in Smithy Door were without exception ancient, a few were dilapidated and in a bad state of repair, but most of them were in a fit state

The Market Place, 1823
(Procter, *Memorials of Manchester Streets*)

of preservation, whilst a few were picturesque, and superior as specimens of the black and white style of architecture to anything that we have today [1906].

(Swindells, *Manchester Streets*)

How the place got its title is one of those legends impossible to prove but tempting to believe:

[A writer in 1788] says: 'There is a tradition that the *Smithy Door* acquired that name on the following laughable occasion. A smith had some money owing him by one of those shirking debtors that would rather expend money in law than pay the debt. The smith kept his accounts in his own way with chalk on the back of the smithy door . . . The debtor was sued at the Hundred Court of Salford, and challenged the smith to produce his books; the smith obtained permission to fetch his book, and entered the court with the door on his back, amidst the loud applause of all present. In short, the smithy door was

allowed to be a good book in law, which cast his antagonist, and gave name to this street, where the smith then lived.'

(Darbyshire, *The Book of Olde Manchester*)

Swindells, writing in 1906, imagined Smithy Door a hundred years previously:

The first [building] that draws our special attention is a tavern kept by widow Wilmott . . . In 1800 the premises were occupied by J. R. Saunders, importer of Irsh linen, but four years later we find Mrs Wilmot in occupation, and there she and her family remained for nearly forty years . . . Next door . . . was the shop of Jacob Williamson, or Old Jacob as he was oftener called. Here was to be seen a curious assortment of books, rare plates, masks, swords, and other stage properties. Many were the scarce books and prints that passed through his hands, and his shop was for many years the resort of the bibliophiles of the town.

(*Manchester Streets*)

Right: The Sydall Residence, Smithy Door
(Darbyshire, *A Book of Oldce Manchester*)
Below: Deakin's Entire, photograph *c.*1866
(Chethams, Assheton Tonge Collection)

'it seems a pity that such an interesting example
should have to give way to the necessities of
modern times. Its downfall commenced in 1808,
when Mary Willmott turned it into a public house;
it became the Vintners' Arms in 1829, and we well
remember it as Sandiford's Vaults and Deakin's
Entire. With its demolition passed away almost the
last relic of the medieval history of Manchester.'
(Darbyshire, *Book of Olde Manchester*)

Manchester was a good place for books, just around the corner was Withy Grove with its kerb-side stalls of book-sellers, one of whom was Elijah Ridings. Known as the 'weaver poet' Ridings was one of a talented group who met at the Sun Inn, also close by. Once believed – wrongly – to be the oldest licensed premises in England, the Sun was as famous in its day as the Bull's Head had been:

. . . our local bards were in the habit of regularly meeting at the ancient hostelry of the Sun, in Long Millgate, for the cultivation of each other's acquaintance, and the linking of themselves together in the bonds of sociability and good fellowship. The scene of their gatherings received in consequence the name of 'The Poets' Corner', and, although comparison be out of the question, there were yet connected

Left: Poet's Corner and 'Sun' Inn, 1842
The Romantic View
(Darbyshire, *Book of Olde Manchester*)

Below: Sun Inn, photograph *c*.1866
The Reality
(Chethams, Assheton Tonge Collection)

with that modest locality, men with talents as genuine, if not as gigantic, as any of those who slumber in its renowned prototype in Westminster Abbey.

(Clubs of Old Manchester, *Literary Club Papers*)

The poets did not have the national success of Mrs. Raffald but enjoyed considerable local popularity. C. J. Prince became, inevitably, the 'Prince of Provincial Poets' and Charles Swain was praised by Robert Southey, the then Poet Laureate: 'If ever man was born to be a poet,

Swain was'. J. H. Nodal, in his obituary of Swain quoted a 'fair specimen' of his 'happiest moments':

*Tripping down the field-path,*
*Early in the morn,*
*There I met my own love,*
*'Midst the golden corn;*
*Autumn winds were blowing,*
*As in frolic chase,*
*All her silken ringlets*
*Backward from her face.*

(Charles Swain *Literary Club Papers*)

John Critchley Prince
*My path has been rugged and hard*
*Through the mazes of life to this hour;*
*Oh! let not my soul be debarr'd*
*From thy smile of beneficent power.*
(Procter, *Memorials of Bygone Manchester*)

Elijah Ridings besides his weaving, poetry and book-selling had a further claim to fame:

Mr Ridings became the last of the Manchester bellmen – an ancient fraternity. The official costume well became the wearer; and 'many's the time and oft' we have listened with pleasure to his sonorous 'O yez! O yez!' His bell, though but a tinkling cymbal, commanded respectful attention and a full audience – the aim and ambition of every legitimate performer. Fortunate officer! whose duties were ever agreeable.

(Procter, *Memorials of Manchester Streets*)

The bellman's office disappeared, as did all these remnants of Manchester's romantic past. Smithy

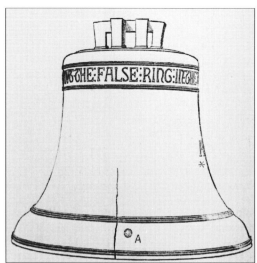

The Great Hour Bell, Town Hall, Manchester. 'The bell first began to give "note of time" on the first of January, 1879, and up to 20 May, 1880, it had been struck with ponderous hammer nearly 79,000 blows . . . The great clock-bell now [1881] hangs cracked and useless in the lantern of the tower; and the above diagram will serve to show the position and extent of the fracture.'
(*Palatine Notebook*)

Door, the Bull's Head, the Sun Inn, the Market Place, Newton's, all fell to the demands of 're-development' from the end of the eighteenth century onwards.

Let the 'Prince of Provincial Poets' voice the appeal of the lost charm of old Manchester, seen through a typically nostalgic haze, to the sound of Manchester's bells.

*Hark, sweetly pealing in the arch of heaven,*
*The mingled music of the Sabbath bells;*
*A time of varying harmony is driven,*
*In gentle wavelets, over streams and dells;*
*Now 'tis a melting cadence – now it swells*
*Full, rich, and joyous on the enamoured ear;*
*While through the wondrous halls where Memory dwells,*
*A thousand visions of the past career,*
*A thousand joys and griefs in dreamy forms appear.*

(Quoted in Procter, *Memorials*)

# 'The Manchester Habit'

The 'greate cloathing towne' of the Middle Ages had developed almost beyond recognition by the nineteenth century. Kohl had 'fled swiftly away on mighty wings of steam' from 'busy, wealthy, populous young Manchester'. He left on a damp, foggy morning as the population went to work:

> In long rows on every side, and in every direction, hurried forward thousands of men, women, and children. They spoke not a word, but huddling up their frozen hands in their cotton clothes, they hastened on, clap, clap, along the pavement to their dreary and monotonous occupations.
>
> (*Ireland, Scotland and England*)

But the changes to the city had been brought about by the very energy of the people. Judge Parry was struck by this characteristic:

> For Manchester is the place where people do things . . . 'Don't talk about what you are going to do – do it.' That is the Manchester habit. And in the past through the manifestation of this quality the word Manchester became a synonym for energy and freedom, and the right to do and to think without shackles.
>
> (*What the Judge Saw*)

The people themselves were the spirit of the city, a sentiment found in *Cloudrifts over cottonopolis*, a novel written in 1911:

> . . . if you really want to know Manchester, Sunday is precisely the time when some of your most important investigations must be made . . . If you wish to see how beautiful our maligned city can look, . . . get up when everybody else is in bed.
>
> I shall never forget the weird charm of Manchester as I saw it when I came in by train at five o'clock one Sunday morning,

and walked up the deserted streets. I saw a dozen things I had never noticed before.

'Just so,' put in Stafford. 'I never noticed that there was a hill in Market Street till I had to walk up it one morning in the early hours. The fact is that ordinarily you can't see the city for the people.'

'Yes,' I added. 'but when I spoke just now of the city, it was the people I meant. It is the human interest of Manchester that holds me. Now, in this great thoroughfare there are few people about at present, but when we come back to-night it will be swarming with life . . . Between eight and ten o'clock, there you will find them in their thousands, mostly young men and girls, sometimes rows of them, linked arm-in-arm, sweeping the pathway, and overflowing into the roads . . .

In spite of all the deprivations, Mancunians had long held an affection for their grimy town often expressed in literature, epitomised perhaps by Harrison Ainsworth's Cottonborough – 'with all its ugliness, and all its faults-and they are many-I love it well.' Mrs Gaskell writes of a city which the labourers, too, hold in affection:

> Far, far away in the distance on that flat plain you might see the motionless cloud of smoke hanging over a great town; and that was Manchester! dear, busy, earnest, working, noble Manchester; where their children had been born (and perhaps where some lay buried,) where their homes were, where God had cast their lives, and told them to work out their destiny.
>
> (Gaskell, *Libby Marsh's Three Eras*)

The population were known for their 'direct' way of talking. Nathaniel Hawthorne, visiting the Art Exhibition of 1853, recorded his impressions:

Speaking of the former rudeness of manners, now gradually refining away, of the Manchester people, Judge —— said that, when he first knew Manchester, women, meeting his wife for the first time in the street, would take hold of her dress and say, 'Ah, three and sixpence a yard!' The men are very rough after the old Lancashire fashion . . . It is singular that the great Art-Exhibition should have come to pass in the rudest great town in England.

(*Complete Works*)

The Judge's successor fifty years later expressed the same opinion:

But the truth compels me to say that my memory of the first aspect of Manchester was a scene of hustle, roughness, and uncouthness rather depressing to a stranger in a strange land not to the manner born. I discovered before long the kindness of heart and the real sense of independence that underlies and is the origin of the Manchester manner.

(Parry, *What the Judge saw*)

Perhaps all these qualities are summed up in the person of Mr Josiah Vacueray, 'the Man from Manchester':

I suppose that all men are more or less proud of their birthplaces. But your Manchester man, above others, seems proud of his. Nor is this pride unjustified, for Manchester in itself is a city to be proud of, and the average middle-class Manchester man is generally an upright, fair-dealing, thoroughly business-like, shrewd, and open hearted fellow. Blunt speech and frank-speaking, he strikes you at once as straightforward and reliable. And if you attempt any double-dealing with him then you find that you have caught a Tartar, for your true Manchester man hates chicanery. He is not suspicious as a rule. By instinct and by nature he is very hospitable. He is a staunch friend, but can also be a bitter enemy.

('Donovan', *The Man from Manchester*)

Writing at the turn of the century, Judge Parry

Young Manchester
(*Punch*, 1844)

recorded that there were many who thought Manchester 'played out'. The Judge disagreed. Richard Cobden, he reported, said, ' all obstacles to fortune with which I am impeded will (nay *shall*) yield if assailed with energy.' This Parry believed was the 'true Manchester spirit and it lives on today'. Parry's vision of the future for the city is perhaps as apt today:

. . . for this I can prophecy − it is information, not a tip − that if there is to be a Manchester at all some hundreds of years hence it will be a city without smoke, its people will be healthy and handsome, its Pharisees will be fewer, and all will breathe pure air and walk clean streets, and when a citizen's day's work is done he will be found angling for trout in the church pool with a better chance of success than he would have today.

But these futures depend on the good Genie of Manchester winning the battles of today. For when energy, freedom, and the power to do things depart from Manchester she will become 'as an oak whose leaf fadeth, and as a garden that hath no water.'

(*What the Judge Saw*)

# Bibliography

[ ] indicate the Portico catalogue reference.

## Chethams Archives

Assheton Tonge Collection
Langton Scrapbook
Manchester Scrapbook
Newspaper Collection
  *Manchester Chronicle*
  *Manchester Mercury*
  *Courier*
  *British Volunteer*

Joseph Adshead, *Prisons and Prisoners* (London, 1845) [Kf 9]

—— Alfred Arnold's Choice (London [n. d.]) [N.W. Fiction]

J. M. D. Aiken, *A description of the County from thirty to forty miles around Manchester* (London, 1795) [Ug 11]

W. H. Ainsworth, *The Leaguer of Lathom*, 3 vols (Manchester, 1876) [Bd 43]

—— Mervyn Clitheroe (London, 1857) [N.W. Fiction]

Anglers' Evenings Papers, by members of the Manchester Anglers Association (Manchester, 1880) [Nh 9]

*Annual Register* (London, 1763) [Qa 8]

Prof. D. T. Ansted, *Water and Water Supply* (London, 1878) [Dp 13]

R. A. Arnold, *The Cotton Famine* (London, 1864 [Kn 11]

John Ashton, *Social Life in the Reign of Queen Anne*, 2 vols (London, 1882) [Vo 114]

Joseph Aston, *A Picture of Manchester* (Manchester 1816) [U supp]

*A Picture of Manchester*, 3rd edn (Manchester [n.d.])

—— The Lancashire Gazetteer, 2nd edn (London, 1822) [Yd 28] (Chethams)

W. E. A. Axon, *Lancashire Gleanings* (Manchester and London, 1883) [Ui 42]

—— The Ancoats Skylark (Manchester, 1894) [A supp]

—— Annals of Manchester (Manchester, 1886) [Ui 60]

Edward Baines, *History, Directory & Gazetteer of the County Palatine of Lancaster* (The Directory Department by W. Parson), 2 vols (Liverpool, 1825) [Yd 3]

—— The History of the County Palatine and Duchy of Lancaster (London, 1836) [Un 3]

*Bannermans Year Book* (Manchester, 1903) [By permission of Adrian Wilson]

T. W. Barlow, *Cheshire and Lancashire Historical Recorder* (Manchester and London, 1855) [Uk 27]

'Tim Bobbin', *The Complete Works of Tim Bobbin* (Manchester, 1862) [Of 2]

Ben Brierly, *Daisy Nook Sketches* (Manchester, 1882) [N.W. Fiction]

Alfred Buxton, *Rush-Bearing* (Manchester, 1891) [U supp]

Richard Buxton, *A Botanical Guide to the Flowering Plants . . . within 16 miles of Manchester* (Manchester, 1849) [Cc 10]

John Byrom, *Private and Literary Remains of John Byrom*, 2 vols (C.S.) (Manchester, 1857) [Ub 1 43–44]

William Camden, *Britannia or a chorographical description of the flourishing kingdoms of England, Scotland and Ireland*, 2nd edn, enlarged by Richard Gough, 3 vols (London, 1806) [Uf 2]

R. Chambers [ed.], *Book of Days*, 2 vols (London [n.d.]) [Wb 39]

Chetham Society Remains Historical & Literary (C.S.) (Manchester, 1862) [Ub 1 57]

H. Cholmondeley-Pennell, *Fishing* (London, 1885) [Nf 34]

Church Wardens Accounts in Chetham Miscellanies (Manchester, 1871) [Ul 80]

S. R. Clarke, *The New lancashire Gazetteer or Topographical Dictionary* (London, 1830) [Yd 4]

*Clouddrifts over Cottonopolis, A series of sketches by an observer* (London, 1911) [U supp]

George Condy, *An argument for placing factory children within the pale of the law* (London, 1833) [Zo 1 38(16)]

Constables' Accounts of the Manor of Manchester, 3 vols (Manchester, 1892) [Pm 6]

J. Corbett, *The River Irwell* (Manchester, 1907) [U supp]

Court Leet Records of the Manor of Manchester, 4 vols (Manchester, 1884) [Pm 5]

W. G. Craven, Earl of Suffolk, *Racing and Steeple Chasing* (London, 1886) [Nf 38]

W. R. Credland, *Days Off Pen and Pencil sketches in Lancashire, Cheshire, Derbyshire, Yorkshire and elsewhere* (Manchester, 1898) [M Supp]

James Croston, *Nooks and Corners of Lancashire and Cheshire* (Manchester, 1882) [Uk 55]

——- *County Families of Lancashire & Cheshire* (Manchester, 1887) [U supp]

J. S. Crowther, *An architectural history of the Cathedral Church of Manchester* (Manchester, 1893) [Uo 28]

*Daddy's Bobby* (Manchester, [n.d.]) [N. W. Fiction]

J. T. Danson, *On the area and population of the Manchester District*, See Transaction of the Historic Society [Uc 34]

A. Darbyshire, *The Book of Olde Manchester and Salford* (Manchester, 1887) [Chethams]

'A Delver', *From dark to light* (Manchester and London, 1885) [N.W. Fiction]

'Donovan Dick', *The Man from Manchester* (London, [n.d.]) [N.W. Fiction]

J. P. Earwaker (ed.), *Local Gleanings*, 2 vols (Manchester, 1875–1879) [U supp]

Thomas Ellison, *A Handbook of the Cotton Trade* (London, 1858) [Kk 21]

Don Manuel Alvarez Espriella, *Letters from England*, 3 vols (London, 1808) [by Robert Southey] [Ml 32]

John Evans, *Lancashire Authors and Orators* (London, 1850) [With kind permission of Eddie Cass]

Everett, *Everett's Manchester Guide* (Manchester, 1840) [Chethams]

Factories Inquiry Commission, *First report of the central board . . . as to the employment of children in factories*, For the House of Commons (London, 1833) [Yb 19]

Factories Inquiry Commission, *Supplementary part of the central board . . . as to the employment of children in factories*, Part ii, For the House of Commons (London, 1834) [Yb 19]

W. Fairbairn, *Remarks on Canal Navigation* (London, Edinburgh, Glasgow & Manchester, 1831) [Wf 12]

W. N. Fairholt, *Costume in England* (London, 1846) [Wl 5]

Lt. Col. H. F. Fishwick, *A History of Lancashire* (Manchester, 1894) [U supp]

——- *The Lancashire Library* (Warrington, 1875) [Yc 68]

Lt. Col. H. F. Fishwick & Rev. P. H. Ditchfield, *Memorials of Old Lancashire* (London, 1909) [U supp]

N. J. Frangopolu (ed.), *Rich Inheritance* (Manchester, 1962) [U supp]

Thomas Fuller, *The History of the Worthies of England*, 2 vols (London, 1811) [Fw 30]

Mrs E. Gaskell, *Life in Manchester: Libby March's Three Eras* (Manchester, 1847 reprinted 1968) [Writing as Cotton Mather Mills] [N.W. Fiction]

[Richard Gough], *British Topography* (London, 1780) [Um 6]

Gregson, *Portfolio of Fragments relative to the History and Antiquities of the County Palatine* (Liverpool, 1824) [Up 5]

Leo H. Grindon, *Lancashire: Brief Historical and Descriptive Notes* (London, 1882) [Uq 14]

——- *Country Rambles, and Manchester Walks and Wild Flowers* (London, 1882) [Cv 86]

Francis Grose and Thomas Astle, *The Antiquarian Repertory: A Miscellaneous Assemblage of Topography, History, biography, Customs and Manners*, 2 vols (London, 1807) [Wi 8]

Richard Guest, *A Compendious History of the Cotton-Manufacture with a disproval of the claim of Sir Richard Arkwright to the invention of its ingenious machinery* (Manchester, 1823) [Kk 2]

Joseph J. Gurney, *Notes on a visit made to some of the prisons in Scotland and the North of England in company with Elizabeth Fry; with some general observations on the subject of prison discipline* (London, 1819) [Kb 35]

John Harland, *Collectanea* (C.S.), Volume 1 (Manchester, 1866) [Ub 1 68]

——- *Collectanea*, Volume 2 (Manchester, 1870) [Ub 1 72]

——- *Ballads and Songs of Lancashire* (London, 1865) [Ab 58]

J. Harland (ed.), *Mamcestre* (C. S.) (Manchester, 1861) [Ub 1 53/56/58]

——- *Volume of Court Leet Records, A* (C.S.) (Manchester, 1844) [Ub 1 63]

Harland and Wilkinson, *Lancashire Folklore* (London, 1867) [Wf 36]

Nathaniel Hawthorne, *Complete Works*, 12 vols (London, 1883) [Oc 7]

Sir George Head, *A Home Tour through the manufacturing districts of England* (London, 1836) [Mo 16]

Henry Heginbotham, *Stockport: Ancient and Modern*, 2 vols (London, 1892) [Uo 14]

Michael Hennell, *The Deans and Canons of Manchester Cathedral 1840–1948* [No publishing details] [U supp]

Samuel Hibbert, *History of the Collegiate Church*, See Whatton [Un 8]

*History of the Manchester ship Canal from its inception to its completion with personal reminiscences by Sir Bosdin Leech*, 2 vols (Manchester, 1907) [U supp]

James Hogg, *The Jacobite Relics of Scotland*, 2nd series (Edinburgh and London, 1821) [Ae 25]

Richard B. Howard, *An inquiry into the Morbid Effects of Deficiency of Food chiefly with reference to their occurrence amongst the destitute poor* (London, 1839) [Dk 17]

James Hunnewell, *Englands Chronicle in Stone* (London, 1886) [Wa 57]

Chev. De Johnstone, *Memoirs of the Rebellion in 1745 and 1746* (London, 1820) [Vd 40]

James P. Kay, *The Moral and Physical conditions of the Working Classes* (Manchester, 1832) [Zo 1 42(2)]

J. G. Khol, *Ireland, Scotland and England* (London, 1844) [Mf 4]

*Lass o' Lowries* (Manchester, [n.d.]) [N. W. Fiction]

John Leland, *The Itinerary of John Leland, the Antiquary*, 9 vols (Oxford 1769–1770) [Ud 3]

James Logan, *The Scottish Gael, or Celtic manner*, 2 vols (London, 1831) [Vb 33]

C. J. Longman and Col. H. Walrand, *Archery* (London, 1894) [Nf 49]

Benjamin Love, *Manchester as it is* (Manchester and London, 1839) [U supp]

*Manchester Directory* (Manchester, 1824) [U supp]

*Manchester Historical Recorder Being an analysis of the . . . history of Manchester* (Manchester, 1875) [Ui 29]

*Manchester Literary Club Transactions* (Manchester, 1875–1903), Index and Catalogue (1903) [Pm 5]

*Manchester Royal Exchange Directory* (Manchester, 1903) [U supp]

*Manchester Quarterly*, volume 8 (Manchester, 1889) [Qr 6]

Hugh Miller, *First impressions of England and its people* (London, 1847) [Uk 9]

*Momus Manchester Evening News Supplement* [Chethams]

*Palatine Notebooks, for the intercommunication of Antiquaries . . . into the history and literature of the counties of Lancaster, Cheshire . . .*, 3 vols (Manchester, 1881–1883) [V supp]

Chev. F. M. G. de Pambour, *A Practical Treatise on Locomotive Engines upon Railways* (London, 1836) [Dd 5]

Rev. R. Parkinson, *The Old Church Clock* (Manchester, 1843) [Bo 90]

His Honour Judge E. A. Parry, *What the Judge Saw* (London, 1912) [F supp]

Richard W. Procter, *Memorials, of Bygone Manchester with glimpses of the environs* (Manchester and London, 1880) [Uk 52]

—— *Memorials of Manchester Streets* (Manchester, 1874) [Uk 51]

*Punch* (London, 1844, 1859) [Ql 10]

James Ralston and Others, *Old Manchester* (Manchester, 1875) [Ue 7]

B. A. Redfern, *A City Idyll*, see Manchester Literary Club

J. Williamson Redfern, *Art in Manchester*, Manchester Literary Club vol. 32 (Manchester, 1913)

Reports of Commissioners, *The First Annual Report of the Poor Law Commissioners* (London, 1836) (By permission of Ann Brooks)

*Report on the Infirmary and Dispensary in Manchester* (Manchester, 1815) [Zo 1–38(6)]

Josiah Ricraft, *A Survey of Englands Champions and Truths Faithful Patriots* (London, 1647) [Facsimile, 1830] [Sl 4]

John Roby, *Traditions of Lancashire and Cheshire*, 2 vols (London, 1871) [V supp]

*Rules and Regulations for the conduct of the traffic and for the guidance of the Officers and Men in the service of the London and North-Western Railway Company* (London, 1849) [K supp]

Charles E. B. Russell, *Manchester Boys Sketches of Manchester lads at work and play* (Manchester, 1905) [U supp]

George Saintsbury, *Manchester* (London, 1887) [Ui 45]

W. A. Shaw, *Manchester Old and New*, 3 vols (Manchester, 1894) [U supp]

M. Sherman, *Athletics and Football* (London, 1887) [Nf 36]

A. Sinclair and W. Henry, *Swimming* (London, 1893) [Nf 45]

J. T. Slugg, *Reminiscences of Manchester Fifty Years Ago* (Manchester, 1881) [U supp]

Samuel Smiles, *Lives of the Engineers*, 2 vols (London, 1861) [Fx 55]

Sarah Smith, see Stretton

R. Southey, see Don Manuel Alvarez Espriella

'Stonehenge', *British Rural Sports* (London, 1871) [Nc 40]

Hesba Stretton, *Pilgrim Street* (London, 1862) [Also published as Sarah Smith] [N.W. Fiction]

William Stukeley, *Itinerarum Curiosum* (London, 1776) [Ug 4]

John Randal Swann, *Lancashire Authors: A series of biographical sketches* (St Anne's, 1924) (By kind permission of Eddie Cass)

T. S. Swindells, *Manchester Streets and Manchester Men* (Manchester, 1st Series 1906, 2nd Series 1907, 5th Series 1908) [U supp]

Herbert Taylor, *Three Incidents*, Manchester Literary Club vol. 39 (Manchester, 1913) [Pm 5]

D. C. Thomson, *The Life and Works of Thomas Bewick* (London, 1882) [Fz 362]

Walter Tomlinson, *Bye-ways of Manchester Life* (Manchester, 1887), (Chethams)

Tracts relating to the Civil War (C.S.) (Manchester, 1844) [Ub 1 2]

Burnett W. Tracy, *Port of Manchester* (Manchester, 1901) [U supp]

*Transactions of the Historic Society of Lancashire and Cheshire*, vol. 8 (Manchester, 1856) [Uc 34]

Andrew Ure, *The Philosophy of Manufacturers* (London, 1835) [Kk 10]

*Vegetable Substances: materials of manufactures* (London, 1833) [Kk 16]

Thomas W. Watkin, *Roman Lancashire; or, a description of Roman remains in the county palatine of Lancashire* (Liverpool, 1883) [Uo 30]

Edwin Waugh, *Poems and Songs* (Liverpool and Oldham, 1889) [B Supp]

W. R. Whatton (ed.), *History of the Collegiate Church*, vols 1 and 2 (of 3) (Manchester, 1830) [Un 8]

—— *History of the Foundations in Manchester of Christs College, Chetham's Hospital and the Free Grammar School*, vol. 3 (Manchester, 1833) [Un 8]

John Whitaker, *History of Manchester*, 2 vols (London, 1771–1775) [Un 11]

W. B. Woodgate, *Boating* (London, 1888) [Nf 46]

T. L. Worthington, *An historical account and illustrated description of the Cathedral Church* (Manchester, 1884) [Wb 48]

Thomas Wright, *Homes of Other Days* (London, 1871) [Wg 42]

Arthur Young, *A Six Months Tour through the North of England*, 4 vols (London, 1770) [Dn 42]

The Portico Library is a private subscription library founded in 1806. Further information may be obtained from the Librarian: 57 Mosley Street, Manchester, telephone 0161 236 6785.